50 Content Area Strategies for Adolescent Literacy

Douglas Fisher
San Diego State University

William G. Brozo
George Mason University

Nancy Frey
San Diego State University

Gay Ivey
James Madison University

PEARSON
Merrill
Prentice Hall

Upper Saddle River, New Jersey
Columbus, Ohio

Library of Congress Cataloging in Publication Data

50 content area strategies for adolescent literacy / by Douglas Fisher ... [et al.].
    p. cm.
  Includes bibliographical references.
  ISBN 0-13-174544-1
    1. Reading (Secondary) 2. Content area reading. I. Title: Fifty content area strategies
for adolescent literacy. II. Fisher, Douglas

  LB1632+
  428.4971'2–dc22

                                                        2007041966

Vice President and Executive Publisher: Jeffery W. Johnston
Senior Editor: Linda Ashe Bishop
Senior Development Editor: Hope Madden
Senior Production Editor: Mary M. Irvin
Design Coordinator: Diane C. Lorenzo
Senior Editorial Assistant: Laura Weaver
Production Coordination and Text Design: Amy Gehl, Carlisle Editorial Services
Cover Designer: Candace Rowley
Cover Images: SuperStock
Production Manager: Pamela D. Bennett
Director of Marketing: David Gesell
Marketing Manager: Darcy Betts Prybella
Marketing Coordinator: Brian Mounts

This book was set in Universe by Carlisle Publishing Services. It was printed and bound by Banta. The cover was printed by Coral Graphic Services, Inc.

Pearson Education Ltd.
Pearson Education Singapore Pte. Ltd.
Pearson Education Canada, Ltd.
Pearson Education—Japan

Pearson Education Australia Pty. Limited
Pearson Education North Asia Ltd.
Pearson Educación de Mexico, S.A. de C.V.
Pearson Education Malaysia Pte. Ltd.

10 9 8 7 6 5 4 3 2 1
ISBN: 0-13-174544-1

Acknowledgments

We would like to begin by thanking Doug Williams, Rita ElWardi, Lee Mongrue, and Christine Johnson for their help as part of the literacy leadership team. Our deep thanks also go out to the teachers at Hoover High School.

When this book was being developed, we got great advice from our exceptional editors Linda Bishop and Hope Madden, as well as from our reviewers: Hazel A. Brauer, *University of San Francisco*; Kouider Mokhtari, *Miami University*; and David G. Petkosh, *Harrisburg Area Community College*.

TEACHER PREP

MERRILL PRENTICE HALL

Teacher Preparation Classroom

Your Class. Their Careers. Our Future. Will your students be prepared?

We invite you to explore our new, innovative and engaging website and all that it has to offer you, your course, and tomorrow's educators! Organized around the major courses pre-service teachers take, the Teacher Preparation site provides media, student/teacher artifacts, strategies, research articles, and other resources to equip your students with the quality tools needed to excel in their courses and prepare them for their first classroom.

This ultimate on-line education resource is available at no cost, when packaged with a Merrill text, and will provide you and your students access to:

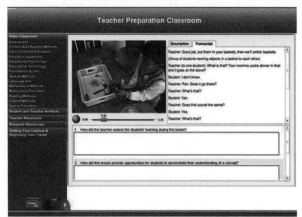

Online Video Library. More than 150 video clips—each tied to a course topic and framed by learning goals and Praxis-type questions—capture real teachers and students working in real classrooms, as well as in-depth interviews with both students and educators.

Student and Teacher Artifacts. More than 200 student and teacher classroom artifacts—each tied to a course topic and framed by learning goals and application questions—provide a wealth of materials and experiences to help make your study to become a professional teacher more concrete and hands-on.

Research Articles. Over 500 articles from ASCD's renowned journal *Educational Leadership*. The site also includes Research Navigator, a searchable database of additional educational journals.

Teaching Strategies. Over 500 strategies and lesson plans for you to use when you become a practicing professional.

Licensure and Career Tools. Resources devoted to helping you pass your licensure exam; learn standards, law, and public policies; plan a teaching portfolio; and succeed in your first year of teaching.

Contents

Introduction

The four of us have spent a significant amount of our professional lives helping teachers help adolescents read more and read better. We have learned a great deal both as teachers and as teacher educators spending time in real classrooms with real students. The examples in this book have been taken from the classrooms we have been privileged to be a part of. We wholeheartedly thank the administrators, teachers, and students who welcomed us into their worlds.

Literacy is key to success in school and throughout life. When we started in this profession, we were told, "All teachers are teachers of reading." We challenge that assumption (e.g., Brozo & Simpson, 2007; Fisher & Ivey, 2005), having altered our thinking to accept that reading, writing, speaking, listening, and viewing are *all* ways that humans learn. As such, every teacher needs to use strategies that allow students to engage in all of these literacy processes. Although this change might seem minor or simply semantic, it represents a conceptual shift from "teaching reading" to using the vast knowledge base about literacy to inform teaching in very classroom. To help you undertake this challenge we have gathered 50 effective content literacy strategies to share with you.

HOW WERE THE STRATEGIES CHOSEN?

We began with three criteria for selecting strategies:

1. **Research Base.** We focus our attention on instructional strategies that work. You'll notice that we introduce each strategy by sharing research evidence.
2. **Usefulness.** We focus on strategies that classroom teachers actually use. While there may be hundreds of evidence-based strategies, some of them are simply too complex, require too much time, or cannot be implemented with groups of students. We did not select those strategies. Rather, we collected strategies we have used successfully, those our colleagues have used successfully, and others we've witnessed in the many dynamic classrooms we've been honored to observe.
3. **Content Area Appropriateness.** Given our understanding that strategies must be transportable—that is, be used by the student throughout his or her day—we selected strategies that could be used in every content area: math, science, social studies, English, visual and performing arts, family and consumer sciences, ROTC, industrial arts, physical education, graphic design, web design, and so on—the classes that our middle and high school students attend.

HOW IS THIS INFORMATION ORGANIZED?

The 50 strategies are organized alphabetically. Ideally this organization will make it easier for you to find the strategies again as the need arises.

The alphabetical structure might be most convenient for you once you become familiar with the strategies, but in the meantime you may need another guide to finding the strategy you need. For that reason the inside cover of the book categorizes the strategies by use before, during, and after reading. Although many strategies are appropriate in more than one situation, this list identifies the most common classroom usage.

Strategies themselves are organized predictably for ease of use.

- Each begins with an introduction that includes a brief review of the research.
- The introduction is followed by step-by-step implementation guidelines.

- Classroom examples further illustrate the successful implementation for each strategy.
- References and graphics, tables, and figures are used when appropriate.

Literacy Focus

⬭ Before Reading	⬭ Fluency
⬭ During Reading	⬭ Comprehension
⬭ After Reading	⬭ Vocabulary
	⬭ Writing
	⬭ Oral Language

A graphic on the front page of each strategy identifies the literacy focus using the strategy before, during, or after a lesson. It also identifies the literacy component that the strategy covers, such as fluency, comprehension, vocabulary, writing, or oral language.

We invite you into the wonderful world of teaching adolescents with content literacy strategies that allow them to develop both their understanding of the content as well as their ability to read, write, speak, listen, and view.

References

Brozo, W. G., & Simpson, M. L. (2007). *Content literacy for today's adolescents: Honoring diversity and building competence* (5th ed.). Upper Saddle River, NJ: Merrill/Prentice Hall.

Fisher, D., & Ivey, G. (2005). Literacy and language as learning in content area classes: A departure from "every teacher a teacher of reading." *Action in Teacher Education, 27*(2), 3–11.

1

Literacy Focus

⬛ Before Reading   ⬜ Fluency
⬜ During Reading   ⬛ Comprehension
⬜ After Reading   ⬛ Vocabulary
                       ⬜ Writing
                       ⬜ Oral Language

Adjunct Displays

Adjunct displays "appear outside of the text, such as pictures, geographic maps, concept maps, graphs, diagrams, outlines, advance organizers, and so forth" (Robinson, Robinson, & Katayama, 1999, pp. 38–39). There is evidence that these displays of information promote recall of text when used in concert with one another. It is believed that adjunct displays are effective because they provide the learner with two avenues to memory—verbal (the text) and spatial (the placement of information in relation to other facts), and that the spatial and verbal memories work in conjunction with one another (Kulhavy, Lee, & Caterino, 1985).

It is important to note that the effectiveness of adjunct displays does not extend to linear forms, such as outlines, when used with text (Robinson et al., 1999). The authors of this study posit that both the text and the outline appeal to verbal memory, and compete with the finite resources of verbal memory. Thus, retention and recall are limited. This is in contrast to the spatial adjunct displays that are used with text, which can access both verbal and spatial memory. Because they are competing for different memory resources, a "bottleneck" does not develop (Robinson et al., 1999).

So, what are the conditions that support the use of adjunct displays in conjunction with written text?

Effective displays reflect the structure of the information. This may seem obtuse, but it's really not. Consider a topic you know a lot about—probably something you teach. Given a few minutes' time, you could sketch a pretty good representation of the information using visual and structural cues for hundreds of words of text. For example, most science teachers would create a visual representation of the rock cycle by using a circle diagram (see Figure 1.1). Let the structure do some of the work for you.

The graphic organizers given to students should be blank or partially completed. Many teachers routinely provide graphic organizers to students, and they are often featured in text-books as chapter organizers. However, should these be completed, blank, or partially filled in with keywords and phrases? It appears that blank or partially completed graphic organizers promote higher text comprehension compared to those that are completed in advance for students (Katayama & Robinson, 2000). Interestingly, it doesn't seem to matter much whether they're blank or partially completed. The level of recall among participants in this study was similar. This should be comforting news for teachers who feel guilty for giving some students partially completed graphic organizers.

For real learning to occur, students must use the graphic organizer to transform information. The goal of an adjunct display is not to fill it out; that's a worksheet. This visual tool is an external storage device for information. If they're going to be useful, adjunct displays should be used to transform information into verbal or written form. Discussion, retelling, summaries, essays—these represent ways in which students demonstrate that they have made the information their own. Plan activities that necessitate the use of the adjunct display they've worked hard to complete.

Figure 1.1 Rock Cycle

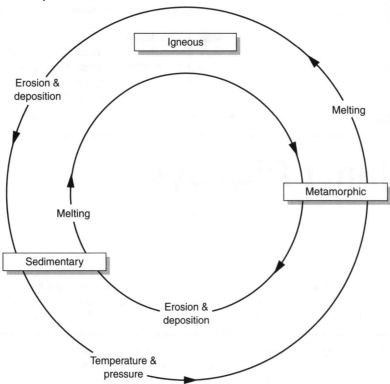

STEP-BY-STEP

1. Select an adjunct display that matches the concepts your students will be reading about. Figure 1.2 lists different types, as well as the purposes for each.
2. Decide whether you will use the selected adjunct display as a blank form or partially completed with keywords and phrases.
3. Distribute the adjunct display and review it with students. Discuss the main ideas or themes of the topic, and explain your reasoning for selecting the type of organizer. Tell students that the passage they are about to read contains information that is structured in a form similar to the adjunct display. Inexperienced students may assume this means a linear organization, so you may need to model how information is extracted from the text.
4. Inform students of the ultimate purpose of the activity. Whether they are to recall and retell information, write a summary, or give an oral presentation, students will perform better when they know the purpose for collecting the information.
5. As students read and complete the adjunct display, circulate and assist students who are having difficulty. It is useful to complete these as a partner activity in order to create an opportunity for oral language development.
6. After students have completed the adjunct display, review the information and transition students to their next task—transforming the information verbally or in written form.

Figure 1.2 Types of Adjunct Displays

Type	Description	Purpose	Example
Concept	Shape-bound words and phrases with connecting lines (see strategy 3, page 10)	Shows relationships between ideas, especially details	
Cycle	Circular maps that show a continuous cycle through the use of arrows	Displays reiterative processes	
Decision tree	Horizontal or vertical lines that radiate	Used to categorize and classify information from general to specific	
Flow diagram	Shape-bound words and phrases combined with arrows to show a process from beginning to end	Shows processes, event sequences, and timelines	
Matrix	Arrangement of words or phrases in a table format that can be read horizontally and vertically	Compares and contrasts concepts; classifies attributes	
Shape map	The overall shape of the map used to represent the concept	Shows hierarchies, movement such as food pyramid	

APPLICATION AND EXAMPLES

Ms. Seymour will be introducing a chapter from the sixth-grade social studies textbook on ancient Egypt. The first section of the chapter deals with the hierarchical structure of Egyptian society. She knows that they need to become familiar with the social classes in order to understand the contrast between the elaborate lifestyle of the pharaoh and his family, and that of the largest group, the unskilled laborers.

She has selected a pyramid adjunct display for two reasons. First, it conveys the rigid hierarchy as well as the relative size of each class. Second, the space of a pyramid is closely associated with ancient Egypt, and she hopes to strengthen the relationship between this new information and the schema, or mental organization system, they have already formed about this culture.

Figure 1.3 Shape Map of Ancient Egyptian Society

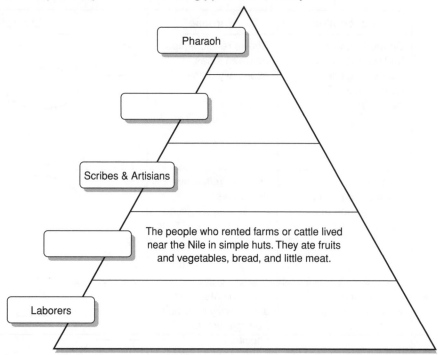

"Class, we're going to be studying life in ancient Egypt, and it's important that you know what life was like for people in every social class. Life could be very, very, good if you were pharaoh. However, it was much more likely that you would be a poor and unskilled worker," she begins. Ms. Seymour distributes the partially completed graphic organizer (see Figure 1.3) and continues. "You'll notice that I have put some of the information in it for you. This is because I want you to have an idea of what other information you should be looking for in the reading."

Ms. Seymour briefly introduces the five social classes and their lifestyles as an advance organizer to the reading. She also tells them that at this time they will be using this information in small groups to create a presentation on a single social class. "You'll want to get lots of good information down on this graphic organizer, because you'll need it to prepare."

She goes on to assign the reading from the textbook and then moves about the classroom to check graphic organizers for accuracy and completeness. As students finish, she has brief conversations with students to check for understanding, and then transitions to a whole-group discussion. For the remainder of the period, Ms. Seymour presents more information about the ancient Egyptian social classes, encouraging students to add details to their graphic organizers. As the bell rings, Ms. Seymour says, "Bring your organizer to class tomorrow—you'll need it for your group presentations!"

References

Katayama, A. D., & Robinson, D. H. (2000). Getting students "partially" involved in note-taking using graphic organizers. *Journal of Experimental Education, 68*(2), 119–133.

Kulhavy, R. W., Lee, B. J., & Caterino, L. C. (1985). Conjoint retention of maps and related discourse. *Contemporary Educational Psychology, 10,* 28–37.

Robinson, D. H., Robinson, S. L., & Katayama, A. D. (1999). When words are represented in memory like pictures: Evidence for spatial encoding of study materials. *Contemporary Educational Psychology, 24,* 38–54.

2

Literacy Focus

■■■ Before Reading   ⊂⊃ Fluency
⊂⊃ During Reading   ■■■ Comprehension
⊂⊃ After Reading   ■■■ Vocabulary
                       ⊂⊃ Writing
                       ⊂⊃ Oral Language

Anticipation Guides

Another strategy that helps instill a situational interest in material in advance of its presentation to students is the anticipation guide (Duffelmeyer & Baum, 1992). A remarkably versatile strategy, anticipation guides can be crafted as preludes to virtually any information source (Merkley, 1996/1997). Another advantage of teaching with anticipation guides is that when crafted appropriately, they prompt students to become active seekers of important information and ideas. Like other effective strategies that begin before students are exposed to the day's material, anticipation guides help sustain attention right through the conclusion of the lesson (Hurst, 2001).

STEP-BY-STEP

There are several different ways of constructing anticipation guides and making them available to middle- and upper-grade students. The following steps will include variations for simplifying the construction and delivery of guides.

1. Begin by reviewing the material to be covered in the day's lesson and identify the most important content. The material or information source might include a textbook, a novel, lecture notes, a DVD, Websites, a guest speaker, or even a field trip.
2. Convert important information and concepts into short statements. These statements should be written in a way that will grab students' attention, challenge preconceived and naïve notions, or arouse curiosity. They do not all have to be factually correct statements, either. In fact, we recommend a combination of statements that can be confirmed by the information source(s) and those that cannot.
3. Present the statements to students. The most common and simplest approach is to write the statements on the board and ask students to copy them. Statements can also be given as a handout, projected on the overhead or from a computer, or even read aloud to students.
4. Give students a response option. For instance, it might be most appropriate to respond either "true" or "false" to the statements. For other statements, "yes" or "no" or "agree" or "disagree" may work best.
5. Ask students to look at each statement using the required response options. Remember, this is done *before* students are provided the information source. Notice for the anticipation guide statements in Figure 2.1 on the topic of cigarette smoking and disease, students are to respond by writing *A* for *agree* or *D* for *disagree* both before and after encountering the material.
6. After individual students initially respond to the statements, have them find a partner and share their responses. This is a critical step because it allows alternative points of

Figure 2.1 Sample Format for Anticipation Guide

Directions: Read each statement carefully and write *A* for *agree* or *D* for *disagree* in the space next to the word *Before.* As you read and hear information related to each statement, decide whether your anticipations need to be changed by placing an *A* or *D* in the space next to the word *After.* Be prepared to explain your choices.

1. The cells of the lungs absorb carbon monoxide more efficiently than oxygen.
Before: _____ After: _____
Explain: _____

   _____

2. Smoking and related diseases kill more people in the United States each year than the total number of Americans killed in World War II.
Before: _____ After: _____
Explain: _____

   _____

view to be expressed, further builds and activates relevant prior knowledge, and heightens anticipation.

7. Gather responses from students. Volunteers can be asked to share whether they agreed or disagreed with the statements. Be sure not to give away answers at this point. Remember, the more eager the students are to find out whether their anticipations are verifiable, the better.

8. Tell students that as they read, listen, or view, they should try to determine whether their initial responses about each statement are supported by the material presented or if they need to be changed. If supported, then students' after-reading and learning response will be the same as their before response. If not supported, their after-reading and learning response will be different than their before response. In either case they should write a brief explanation for their after-reading and learning response based on relevant content from the information source or sources they encounter during the lesson.

9. Present the information source(s). As material is covered, stop periodically and have students discuss with their partners whether they now have relevant information to corroborate or reject their initial anticipations.

10. Finally, ask for volunteers to share both their before- and after-reading and learning responses along with explanations. During sharing, any lingering misconceptions about the anticipation guide statements can be clarified.

APPLICATION AND EXAMPLES

A high school industrial arts teacher was having difficulty getting her students to read the class textbook, especially on topics about which they thought they knew everything, such as managing money. For instance, in the past when covering the chapter on buying a car, her students would resist reading by saying they knew all about the topic. When asked what they already know about purchasing a car, much of what her students say is inaccurate, reflecting incomplete prior knowledge.

To entice her students to read the textbook and help them focus more closely on important information and ideas, the teacher developed the anticipation guide in Figure 2.2 on purchasing a car.

She forms groups of three and has them discuss and debate their answers. Before long, lively and animated conversation erupts throughout the room as students challenge and confirm hunches and assert their experience. The teacher stretches out the anticipation by asking students to take sides based on their responses and conduct a brief debate. By now, they're asking: Who's right?

At this point, the teacher tells the class to begin reading the chapter. She stops students periodically, so they can check the anticipation guide statements and determine whether they need to revise any of them based on the new information.

Figure 2.2 Anticipation Guide for Chapter on Purchasing a Car

Directions Before Reading: Show me what you know about buying a car. Read the statements below and indicate whether you think the statement is true or false in the Before Reading column. Compare your responses with someone sitting next to you. *Directions After Reading:* After reading information related to each statement, decide whether you still think it's true or false. Write information from the chapter that supports your response.				
Statement and support	Before reading True	False	After reading True	False
1. When buying a car it is good to know the dealer cost.				
Support:				
2. The sticker price on the car is the final price.				
Support:				
3. Used cars have a cheaper monthly payment than new cars.				
Support:				
4. Dealer costs are more than retail costs.				
Support:				
5. It is smarter to buy a used car than a new car.				
Support:				
6. Ten percent markup is a reasonable profit for selling a car.				
Support:				
7. The suggested retail price is what the dealer has to sell the car for in order to make a profit.				
Support:				

She concludes by asking individuals to share what was found in the chapter relative to guide statements and point out where supporting information can be found in the text for an after-reading response.

References

Duffelmeyer, R., & Baum, D. (1992). The extended anticipation guide revisited. *Journal of Reading, 35,* 654–656.

Hurst, B. (2001). The ABCs of content area lesson planning: Attention to basics, and comprehension. *Journal of Adolescent & Adult Literacy, 44,* 692–693.

Merkley, D. (1996/1997). Modified anticipation guide. *The Reading Teacher, 50,* 365–368.

3

Literacy Focus

⊖ Before Reading	⊖ Fluency
⬛ During Reading	⬛ Comprehension
⊖ After Reading	⬛ Vocabulary
	⊖ Writing
	⊖ Oral Language

Concept Maps

Graphic organizers are visual displays of information, often arranged in bubbles or squares with connecting lines between them that are used to portray conceptual relationships. Graphic organizers help students comprehend texts by allowing them to transfer texts into visual representations. Alvermann and Van Arnam (1984) noted that graphic organizers such as concept maps prompt students to reread text passages in order to clarify their understanding. Graphic organizers also ensure that students are more active readers (Alvermann & Boothby, 1982), facilitate learning for students who struggle with reading (Lovitt & Horton, 1994), and provide a scaffold for independent reading and writing (James, Abbott, & Greenwood, 2001).

Concept maps are a specific type of graphic organizer and there are several common types. You have already read the information about adjunct displays in Strategy 1 and have some types of visual tools at your disposal. Two additional types are the spider and hierarchy concept maps. The "spider" concept map is created by placing the central factor, theme, or idea in the center of the map and then using lines to indicate the subthemes (see Figure 3.1). The "hierarchy" concept map presents information in descending order of importance. The most important information is placed at the top and information branches out according to the hierarchy (see Figure 3.2).

STEP-BY-STEP

The creation of a concept map first begins with instructional and content decisions you will make for your class. If students are novices to constructing concept maps, teacher modeling will be necessary. As well, you will need to make choices about the content itself and how it might be represented to show the complexities of the topic.

1. Begin by gathering research materials, including textbooks and other supplementary materials used either to prepare for class or as teaching tools. The ideas chosen for use in a concept map should represent critical knowledge for the course, and not just a list of facts strung together.
2. Review the types of concept map formats and select one for use in the lesson. The best way to become acquainted with the formats is to construct some. Focus on what students should glean from this lesson. For example, if understanding how the human eye works is the emphasis of the lesson, a systems map is in order. You may notice many concepts can be represented in more than one way. The human eye might also be represented in a spider map that allows for learners to label the parts and their functions.

Figure 3.1 Spider Concept Map

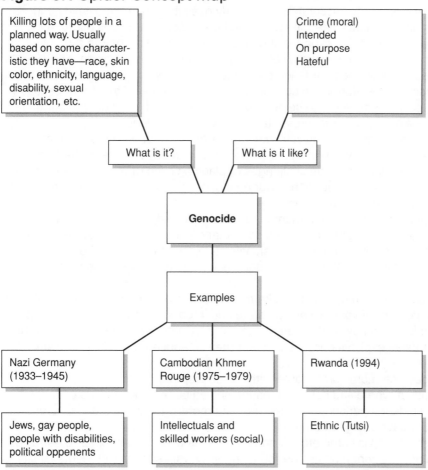

Figure 3.2 Hierarchy Concept Map

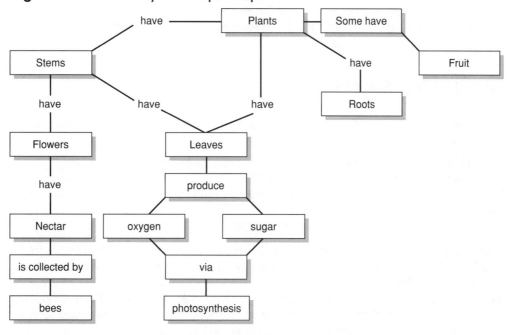

3. After drafting a map, analyze it for clarity and content. In particular, look to see whether the information represented accurately and clearly describes the relationships and interactions of the elements listed. Keep in mind that a concept map is useful for novices to the content. As an expert in the field, you may read more into the information than those with less knowledge would be able to do. Consider showing the map to a colleague who does not teach the subject to see whether he or she can accurately describe the information contained in it. This is a great litmus test because the ultimate goal is for students to be able to transform the information into another form—perhaps a discussion, oral presentation, or written product.

4. Decide whether students will receive a skeleton of the map, or will create the map by hand. An advantage of providing novices with a concept map template is that they won't become frustrated with the challenges of planning each of the components on the page. We've met with frustration in our own classes when a student has run out of space on the page and must begin again.

5. The lesson opening is crucial to students' success in developing a concept map. Inform students at the beginning of the lesson that one of the day's outcomes will be the construction of a concept map. This signals students that they will be attending to two aspects of the lesson—the content itself, as well as the development of the concept map.

6. Use an overhead or data projector to make the map development clear to students. As you teach the content of your lesson, pause to add information to the concept map. Explain your thinking in how you have chosen the information you have written in the map. Without these explanations, the concept map is reduced to a fill-in-the-blank worksheet.

7. As students become more comfortable with the concept map, ask them for suggestions about where and how information should be recorded on the concept map. Inviting student input supports their growing metacognitive awareness about the schema you are developing with them.

8. Once the concept map is completed, it shouldn't be filed in a notebook or folder. The true strength of a concept map can be found in the ways it supports students' ability to transform information. Because the concept map is ultimately a scaffolding device for holding information, students should be challenged to use the tool they have created. Their map can be used to:
   - summarize information with a partner.
   - create a study guide with a small group.
   - provide notes for an extemporaneous speech.
   - write a persuasive essay or report of information.
   - serve as a planning document for a more extensive research report.

APPLICATION AND EXAMPLES

In a world history class, students were reading from a collection of books about World War II, including:

- *World War II: Opposing Viewpoints in World History,* edited by Don Nardo (2005)
- *Rosie the Riveter* by Christine Petersen (2005)
- *The United States in World War II, 1941–1945* by Christopher Collier and James Lincoln Collier (2002)
- *Children During Wartime* by Brenda Williams (2005)

Each group was asked to create a graphic organizer based on the information group members gathered from their collection of books. Jesse and his group created the spider concept map about genocide (see Figure 3.1).

In a science class, students used a hierarchy concept map as they took notes on a film about the components of plants. This served as an introduction to the differences between plant and animal cells. One student's notes are shown in Figure 3.2.

References

Alvermann, D. E., & Boothby, P. R. (1982, September). *A strategy for making content reading successful: Grades 4–6.* Paper presented at the annual meeting of the Plains Regional Conference of the International Reading Association, Omaha, NE. (ED 221 853)

Alvermann, D. E., & Van Arnam, S. (1984, April). *Effects of spontaneous and induced lookbacks on self-perceived high and low ability comprehenders.* Paper presented at the annual meeting of the American Educational Research Association, New Orleans, LA. (ED 246 384)

Collier, C., & Collier, J. L. (2002). *The United States in World War II, 1941–1945.* New York: Benchmark Books.

James, L. A., Abbott, M., & Greenwood, C.R. (2001). How Adam became a writer: Winning writing strategies for low-achieving students. *Teaching Exceptional Children, 33*(3), 30–37.

Lovitt, T. C., & Horton, S. V. (1994). Strategies for adapting science textbooks for youth with learning disabilities. *Remedial and Special Education, 15,* 105–116.

Nardo, D. (Ed.). (2005). *World War II: Opposing viewpoints in world history.* San Diego, CA: Greenhaven Press.

Petersen, C. (2005). *Rosie the riveter.* New York: Children's Press.

Williams, B. (2005). *Children during wartime.* Chicago: Heinemann Library.

4

Dictoglos

Dictoglos is a strategy used to improve students' listening comprehension and oral communication skills (Wajnryb, 1990). A fluent reader reads material aloud as students take notes. The reader rereads the information a few times so that students can add to their notes and obtain a fairly accurate representation of the original material. Following their individual listening, students meet in dyads or groups and talk about the reading, adding to their individual notes.

This approach also helps students focus on their notetaking skills, builds vocabulary, and facilitates content knowledge as they listen for specific information and discuss this information with a partner or small group. As students listen to the same information presented several times, they experience hearing and recording fluent English. As such, dictoglos is also an effective strategy for English language learners (Herrell & Jordan, 2004).

STEP-BY-STEP

Effective dictoglos requires careful planning to select the piece students will write. As well, there is a procedure students will need to be taught so that they are not needlessly anxious about the challenge of capturing all the information.

1. Choose a piece of text that is a rich example of the content being taught. This selection may come from the textbook or other related reading material. If you do not locate any text selection that is satisfactory, consider writing your own. The selection chosen should be appropriate to the language level of the students, and should contain a sufficient amount of academic vocabulary to challenge, but not overwhelm. Shorter pieces are advisable when introducing dictoglos, as students new to the process will not yet possess the listening comprehension strategies dictoglos is intended to build. Nothing succeeds like success, and students who view themselves as capable from the beginning will advance more rapidly than those who struggle from the beginning.

2. Explain the procedure to students before beginning. Tell them that you will read aloud a passage several times for them to write down. The first reading will be a time to listen only. Let them know you will read it two more times, and each time they will write down key words and phrases. They will then work with a partner to reconstruct the text as closely as possible to the original. These partners will meet with another pair and will further refine their passage. Finally, each group will read aloud the new passage and compare it to the original.

3. Read aloud the selected passage, reminding students that this first round is for careful listening. Read the passage at a moderate rate, using pitch, intonation, and phrase boundaries that will help students recall the information.

4. Tell students that you will read the passage two more times, and they should write down key words and phrases. Reread the passage using a similar style of rate and prosody (inflection, intonation, rhythm, etc.) so that each reading becomes increasingly familiar. Do not pause after sentences or key phrases, but rather read the passage in its entirety. Before beginning the third reading, remind students that they should follow their notes and add words and phrases they missed.

5. After the third reading, invite students to work in pairs to co-construct a version of the original text. Encourage them to compare notes to develop a more complete version than they might have written alone.

6. Form groups of four to compare passages, and again write a co-constructed passage. This version is likely to be closer to the original.

7. Ask a member from each group to read aloud their passage before you reread the original text. Lead a class discussion on the students' insights into the degrees of difficulty in portions of the text. As well, ask them to share strategies they used to capture the information. For example, some students write their words and phrases as a double-spaced list, adding new information gleaned from the third reading in the spaces.

APPLICATION AND EXAMPLES

In her English class, Ms. Javier wanted to focus her students on their listening comprehension skills. She also wanted to share the joys of poetry with her students and decided to use the dictoglos strategy as she introduced the poetry of Ogden Nash, specifically the poem "Adventures Of Isabel." You can find the poem in the colorful picture book *Adventures of Isabel* by Ogden Nash, illustrated by James Marshall, or on a variety of websites, including *http://www.burtonsys.com/isabel.htm*.

After explaining the procedure for dictoglos, Ms. Javier read aloud the poem. Finding her "actress within" she shares the poem and its humor with her students. Once they understand the nature of the poem, she reminds them that they are going to write down everything they can remember as she reads it to them again. She rereads the first stanza of the poem twice for the class. During these two read alouds, the students must take notes on what they hear so that they can re-create the text as accurately as possible. Consistent with the dictoglos strategy, Ms. Javier provides her students with a few minutes to write what they remember from the read alouds.

After they have written all that they can remember, students pair up and share what they have written. They add to their own notes from what they hear their partner share. Then two pairs join together and the group of four students try to re-create the first stanza of the poem from their collective papers and notes. By this time, students have reviewed their notes, listened to and read others' notes, and revised their own notes.

When they have completed this process for the first stanza, Ms. Javier repeats the procedure for the second, third, and fourth stanzas of the poem. As students engage in this process, they gain a better understanding of the text structure Nash used and they find it easier to recall words because many of them rhyme.

In completing this lesson, Ms. Javier knows that she has focused her students on listening comprehension, expanded their vocabulary knowledge, and facilitated their notetaking skills. Students gain these skills in a nonthreatening, engaging, and collaborative way.

References

Herrell, A., & Jordan, M. (2004). *Fifty strategies for teaching English language learners* (2nd ed.). Upper Saddle River, NJ: Merrill/Prentice Hall.

Wajnryb, R. (1990). *Grammar dictation*. Oxford, England: Oxford University Press.

5

Directed Notetaking Activity

The directed notetaking activity (DNA) is based on three instructional ideas: the split-page method for structured notetaking (see Strategy 38, "Split-Page Notetaking"); a self-questioning strategy for students to monitor their levels of involvement before, during, and after notetaking; and direct, explicit teaching of the notetaking process (Spires & Stone, 1989). During a directed notetaking activity, students are taught to think about their notetaking skills and behaviors. Students also learn how to study from their notes and how to keep themselves organized for classes.

One of the key features of DNA involves students learning to self-question. Self-questioning is one way that readers engage with texts. In addition, because students are expected to demonstrate what they know on written tests, self-questioning may help students perform better on standardized assessments. Of course, the type and difficulty of the question impacts student understanding and performance. If students regularly self-question using factual recall, they will likely not perform well on tasks or assessments that include comprehension, application, or synthesis of main ideas. Although this may be obvious, it is also important to note that an exclusive focus on application and synthesis may jeopardize students' ability to recall information from reading passages.

The evidence on teaching students how to generate questions as they read and take notes suggests that there are several factors that impact the questions students ask of themselves, including their prior knowledge about the topic, their metacognitive skills, the clarity of instructions, and the amount of practice allowed the student (Armbruster et al., 1991; Keene & Zimmermann, 1997; Kozminsky & Kozminsky, 2001).

STEP-BY-STEP

1. DNA requires that students consider their notetaking behaviors. Figure 5.1 shows a list of guidelines for students before, during, and after notetaking. Thus, the first step is to ensure students pay attention to the skills and strategies they already use to take notes.
2. Students must also become familiar with self-questioning and self-monitoring. Teachers often model these metacognitive approaches for students. As you model DNA on an overhead projector or whiteboard, tell students how you have selected the information you are writing in the notes. Pause to ask questions aloud so that they can be privy to the decisions learners make as they write.
3. Begin by modeling how the page is to be set up. Although this may seem like a simple prospect, it is amazing how many good lessons get derailed at this step. Show students how to fold (but not crease) their note page so that the leading edge is about 2 inches from the left side of the paper. This provides a straight edge to draw a line

Figure 5.1 Notetaking Guidelines

Before notetaking:
1. Have your notebook organized.
2. Have paper and writing instruments ready.
3. Review previous notes.

During notetaking:
1. Use only one side of the paper.
2. Draw a margin about 2 inches from the left edge of the paper.
3. Use the area to the right of the margin line to take notes and leave the left margin blank as you take notes.
4. Skip lines to indicate new ideas.
5. Listen carefully to the information and write down important ideas and details.
6. Use abbreviations such as *w/* for *with* or *w/o* for *without* to save time and keep up with the information being presented.

After notetaking:
1. Review your notes and find the important ideas and supporting details.
2. In the left column, write questions or summary statements about these important ideas and supporting details.
3. Study your notes by covering the right column and trying to answer the questions in the left column. Try to remember as many details as possible.

from top to bottom. Explain that they will take notes to the right of the line they have drawn. (See Strategy 38)

4. As you teach the lesson, pause to allow students to write notes. Remind them to use key words and phrases rather than complete sentences, and to use abbreviations to aid in writing. Encourage them to skip lines to indicate a new idea or topic.
5. After the notetaking portion of the lesson is complete, invite students to review their notes. The left column will now be completed. As students reread their notes, ask them to write questions or summary statements in the corresponding area of the left column. Students may initially have some difficulty with this part of the DNA because they are more concerned with getting the "right" answers in their notes. Remind them that notes are a tool, and that there will be variance among students regarding the questions and summary statements in the left column. If necessary, pose questions to them that scaffold their thinking about the topic.

APPLICATION AND EXAMPLES

"What questions might we ask about Georgia O'Keefe's style, just by looking at this page of text?" Ms. Montoya queries her fine art class as they participate in a prereading activity for the book *Georgia O'Keeffe: The Life of an Artist* by Ray Spangenburg (2002). She knows that creating a skeletal note structure of the text is a powerful prereading skill her students must acquire in order to become effective notetakers and note makers.

Consistent with the DNA process approach, Ms. Montoya wants her students to become familiar with the structure of the text, preview the targeted vocabulary, form questions, question themselves and others, and gain background knowledge from all of the illustrations, photographs, and captions.

With books open, Ms. Montoya and her students skim the text, page by page, as they contribute ideas to the class notes displayed on one of two data projector screens set up at opposite ends of the room. An outline of the chapter takes shape as the class decides on bullets of main ideas, from the headings and subheadings of each page and their discussion notes. Ms. Montoya then leaves empty bullets under each main idea, areas requiring support information, to be completed later as students read books from her collection about this artist.

References

Armbruster, B., Anderson, T., Armstrong, J., Wise, M., Janisch, C., & Meyer, L. (1991). Reading and questioning in content areas. *Journal of Reading Behavior, 23,* 35–59.

Keene, E. O., & Zimmermann, S. (1997). *Mosaic of thought: Teaching comprehension in a reader's workshop.* Portsmouth, NH: Heinemann.

Kozminsky, E., & Kozminsky, L. (2001). How do general knowledge and reading strategies ability relate to reading comprehension of high school students at different educational levels? *Journal of Research in Reading, 24,* 187–204.

Spangenburg, R. (2002). *Georgia O'Keeffe: The life of an artist.* Berkeley Heights, NJ: Enslow Publishers.

Spires, H. A., & Stone P. D. (1989). The directed notetaking activity: A self-questioning approach. *Journal of Reading, 33,* 36–39.

Directed Reading-Thinking Activity

A popular method for creating a focus on critical thinking is the directed reading-thinking activity (Stauffer & Harrell, 1975). The DR-TA, as it is commonly known, is an instructional technique that invites students to make predictions, and then check their predictions during and after the reading. An advantage of the DR-TA is that it assists listeners in clarifying the purpose for the reading. In addition, the DR-TA provides a frame for self-monitoring because the teacher pauses throughout the reading to ask students questions. Because the text is viewed and read by the students as well as the teacher, it is considered to be a form of shared reading (see Strategy 36).

STEP-BY-STEP

Although the steps of a DR-TA may vary slightly in individual practice, the sequence usually consists of the following (Stauffer & Harrell, 1975):

1. *Introduce background knowledge.* Begin the lesson with a discussion of the topic of the reading. Elicit information the students may already know, including personal experiences and prior readings. Discuss the title, cover (if there is one), and any other salient information. Record students' ideas on the board or chart paper.

2. *Make predictions.* Although these predictions can be part of a class discussion, we like to use this as an opportunity to write. Ask questions that invite prediction, such as:
   * What do you expect the main idea of this article will be?
   * From the title, do you anticipate that the author will be for or against?
   * Will this short story have a happy or tragic ending?

   After students have written their predictions, extend their writing further by instructing them to explain what evidence they used to arrive at their predictions.

3. *Read a section of text, stopping at predetermined places in the text. Ask students to check and revise their predictions.* This is a crucial step in DR-TA instruction. Identify where the natural stopping points are, and then ask students to reread their predictions. Let them know they should change their predictions if necessary and cite new evidence that has influenced their opinions. Repeat this cycle several times through the course of the shared reading. Invite them to consider these key questions:
   * What do you know so far from this reading? (summarize)
   * How do you know it? (cite evidence in the text)
   * What do you expect to read next? (predict)

4. *After the reading is completed, use student predictions as a discussion tool.* The beauty of a DR-TA may not be apparent until this step. We have all faced the blank stares and

Figure 6.1 Student Notetaking Form for Directed Reading-Thinking
         Activity

DR-TA for (title): _____

Prediction question(s): _____
_____
_____

Using the title, your own background knowledge, and any other contextual clues, make your
predictions.

Before reading:

During reading:

During reading:

During reading:

After reading:

shuffled silence of adolescents reluctant to respond to discussion questions. However,
when students have written and revised predictions throughout a reading, the tools for
discussion lie waiting for them in their own handwriting. "What did you expect to happen
before we began the reading?" is easily recalled when the student has a record of his or
her thoughts to consult. Another important strategy is embedded in their predictions—it
serves as a track record for their thinking processes. The ability to understand one's own
thinking (metacognition) is viewed as a key to increased comprehension (Fitzgerald,
1983). A sample form for student notetaking using DR-TA is provided in Figure 6.1.

APPLICATION AND EXAMPLES

A directed reading-thinking activity is useful for teaching content while highlighting the strategies good readers use to understand text. For example, Ms. Chen, an eighth-grade social
studies teacher, used an excerpt from the book *Dear Benjamin Banneker* (Pickney, 1998) in a
DR-TA to model the thinking processes while teaching about the contributions of this African

American patriot. She began by introducing the background knowledge necessary to understand the reading. Ms. Chen displayed the reading on an overhead projector and asked students to review the paper copy in front of them.

Ms. Chen: Class, look at the woodcut portrait of the man. What does this woodcut tell you?

James: I think that it shows an old rich guy.

Leah: Yeah, and he probably lived around the time of the Revolutionary War because that's what we're learning about.

Ms. Chen: You are both right. The events in this book take place during the Revolutionary War. Look at the three words I have written on the board. [Ms. Chen asked students to preview key vocabulary she considered essential to understanding the piece—*astronomer* and *surveyor.* She then spoke at length about the meaning of the word *hypocrite.*. She asked students to think about these words and invited the class to consider the first of a series of predictions about what they expected to read.]

Ms. Chen: What do you think the author will write about? What is it that we'll learn from this book?

Kaila: I wonder why the title has "dear" in it—that's from a letter.

Zack: I think the author's gonna tell us how this guy got his money—what he did during the war.

The class then paused for a few minutes while each student wrote a brief prediction about *Dear Benjamin Banneker,* using the form found in Figure 6.1. Ms. Chen then began to read aloud from the first passage (a few paragraphs) while the students followed silently. At the first break, she asked them to think about what they knew so far.

Arturo: Banneker was an astronomer and surveyor. He wrote an almanac for farmers.

Ms. Chen: Yes, Arturo. What evidence do you find in the text for this?

Arturo read the sentences that contained this information. Leah then noted that Banneker was one of the first people to stand up for the civil rights of African Americans. She also noted where she found the information in the reading. Several students underlined these passages on their copies. Finally, Ms. Chen completed the third part of the DR-TA questioning cycle by inviting them to consider what they might read in subsequent passages. Students made several predictions, and Ms. Chen then asked students to revise their written predictions before continuing. As students continued to read, they learned about Banneker's scientific contributions. More important, they came to understand that his significant contribution was a written correspondence he held with Secretary of State Thomas Jefferson, questioning his ownership of slaves. Banneker published his and Jefferson's letters, igniting a firestorm of controversy that raged for decades, eventually leading to the Civil War.

At each break in the reading, Ms. Chen asked her students questions that encouraged them to summarize the text and to cite evidence from the text. She also asked them to revise their predictions based on this new information. At the end of the reading, the students' predictions became the centerpiece of their discussion about Banneker and his role in American history. Ms. Chen reminded her students of the clues they used throughout the reading that allowed them to continually revise their predictions during their reading. In conclusion, she pointed out that good readers do this all the time—they continually think about what they are reading and revise their thinking to better understand what the reading is about and how it either revises or fits into their own background knowledge.

References

Fitzgerald, J. (1983). Helping readers gain self-control over reading comprehension. *The Reading Teacher, 37,* 249–253.

Pickney, A. D. (1998). *Dear Benjamin Banneker.* New York: Voyager Press.

Stauffer, R. G., & Harrell, M. M. (1975). Individualized reading-thinking activities. *The Reading Teacher, 28,* 765–769.

7

Literacy Focus

- ⬭ Before Reading
- ⬛ During Reading
- ⬭ After Reading

- ⬛ Fluency
- ⬛ Comprehension
- ⬭ Vocabulary
- ⬭ Writing
- ⬛ Oral Language

Echo or Choral Reading

Two kinds of support reading—echo reading and choral reading—can be used to help students become more fluent in reading a particular passage (Rasinski et al., 2005). The idea of *echo reading* is that a teacher reads aloud small portions of text to allow students to hear how a text should sound, and then students reread the same portion of text mimicking the fluency and intonation of the teacher. Students continue to "echo" the teacher's reading in subsequent segments until they reach the end of the text. This process may be followed by *choral reading,* in which the teacher and students read simultaneously, with the teacher gradually letting the students take the lead. One of the immediate goals of echo and choral reading is for students to learn to read a particular text independently with fluency and understanding. Many experiences with support reading likely lead to growth in reading fluency.

STEP-BY-STEP

1. Select a piece of text that allows for interesting applications of reading fluency, voice, prosody, phrase boundaries, or intonation.
2. For echo reading, read a section of the text and then invite students to reread the section aloud.
3. For choral reading, either read the section first and then read it with students or read the selection together from the beginning.
4. Once the procedures for echo and choral reading have been established, vary the reading by having half of the class read one sentence with you and then the other half read the next sentence, and so on.
5. If the class is not reading with increased fluency, prosody, or intonation, be explicit in the goal of echo and choral reading. Ask students to "read the punctuation" or "make it sound like talking" or "read with feeling."

APPLICATION AND EXAMPLES

Although improving overall reading fluency is an important goal for reading instruction, it may be hard to imagine why a content area teacher might be interested in echo and choral reading. However, there are instances in which these strategies could become quite useful. For example, echo and choral reading are often used for students who are so inexperienced with reading, even in the later grades, that there is no text they can read independently without frustration (Worthy, Broaddus, & Ivey, 2001). Students who are recent immigrants learning to read, write, and speak English may greatly benefit from this type of support when placed in a regular content area class. For instance, in a seventh-grade science class, students are reading a range of books on animal behaviors and adaptations as part of individual inquiry projects. Luis, who recently immigrated from Mexico, finds most of the books very difficult and stares blankly at the pictures in a book as classmates around him read. However, his teacher capitalizes on the time when other students are engaged in reading to spend some individual time with Luis and the book *Camouflage* (Luhrs, 1996). This book is appropriate for a student at the beginning stages of language learning because of its repetitive pattern:

> What do you see? A fawn. It is hiding in the forest.
> What do you see? A moth. It is asleep on the tree. (pp. 4–5)

To avoid cognitive overload from trying to focus on content, new English vocabulary, and reading all at the same time, it is important for students like Luis to have access to texts like this one that help him concentrate on a few large concepts. Also, texts such as this are useful because the text is supported by what is represented in the accompanying photographs.

Because Luis would have great difficulty on his own with this text, despite its simplicity, his teacher uses a combination of echo and choral reading to support his reading, understanding, and vocabulary. Along the way she can emphasize the concept of animal camouflage as it relates to what students are learning in science class. Here is Luis's teacher's strategy for helping Luis learn from text through support reading:

- First, realizing just how much support Luis needs, she reads the book to Luis in its entirety, stopping along the way to explain certain concepts and ask Luis, as she points to pictures, for the Spanish equivalent of certain important words (e.g., *camouflage*, *lizard*, *tiger*), making this informative for both Luis and his teacher.
- Second, they take a second journey through the book. This time, Luis's teacher asks him to echo each line of text after she reads it. Quickly, Luis learns to read repeated phrases quite fluently and with understanding.
- Third, Luis and his teacher read again, this time in unison. As they read chorally, Luis's teacher gradually lets her voice fade as Luis becomes more confident.
- Fourth, Luis reads the entire book independently. As the new vocabulary begins to make more sense to him, so does the concept of camouflage.

Other books related to the topic that work well for echo and choral reading include the following:

Berger, M., & Berger, G. (2003). *Owls live in trees*. New York: Scholastic.
Berger, M., & Berger, G. (2003). *Snakes live in grass*. New York: Scholastic.
Birchall, B. (1996). *How animals hide*. Bothell, WA: The Wright Group.
Canizares, S. (1998). *Where do insects live?* New York: Scholastic.
Chessen, B. (1998). *Animal homes*. New York: Scholastic.

References

Luhrs, R. J. (1996). *Camouflage*. Bothell, WA: The Wright Group.
Rasinski, T. V., Padak, N. D., McKeon, C. A., Wilfong, L. G., Friedauer, J. A., & Heim, P. (2005). Is reading fluency a key for successful high school reading? *Journal of Adolescent & Adult Literacy, 49*, 22–27.
Worthy, J., Broaddus, K., & Ivey, G. (2001). *Pathways to independence: Reading, writing, and learning in grades 3–8*. New York: Guilford Press.

8

Literacy Focus

⬭ Before Reading   ⬭ Fluency
⬭ During Reading   ⬛ Comprehension
⬛ After Reading   ⬭ Vocabulary
                ⬛ Writing
                ⬭ Oral Language

Exit Slips

Writing at the close of the class period, even in brief formats, can help students reflect on what they have learned and, in a sense, help prepare their minds for continued learning on the topic. Exit slips are a quick and easy way for students to maintain involvement with a lesson even as it ends. In short, students spend several minutes jotting down their thoughts about the lesson, usually responding to some sort of prompt. These are turned in not for a grade, but instead as a way to show students' thinking process. There are no right or wrong answers on exit slips. Teachers can use student exit slips to assess the effectiveness of their teaching and to make decisions about what to revisit, elaborate upon, or bring to a close.

STEP-BY-STEP

Three categories of exit slips are as follows:

1. *Prompts that document learning*

   The three most important things I learned today are . . .
   Today I changed my mind about . . .
   What I would like to tell someone else about what I learned today is . . .

2. *Prompts that emphasize the process of learning*

   Two questions I have about what we did in class today are . . .
   I am confused about . . .
   What I would like to learn next is . . .

3. *Prompts to evaluate the effectiveness of the instruction*

   The thing that helped me pay attention most today was . . .
   The thing that helped me understand most today was . . .
   Something that did not help me learn in class today was . . .

APPLICATION AND EXAMPLES

Mr. Petersen uses exit slips as the "ticket out the door" when his students leave their science class. He provides his students a response paper (see Figure 8.1) on which they can

Figure 8.1 Sample Response Page

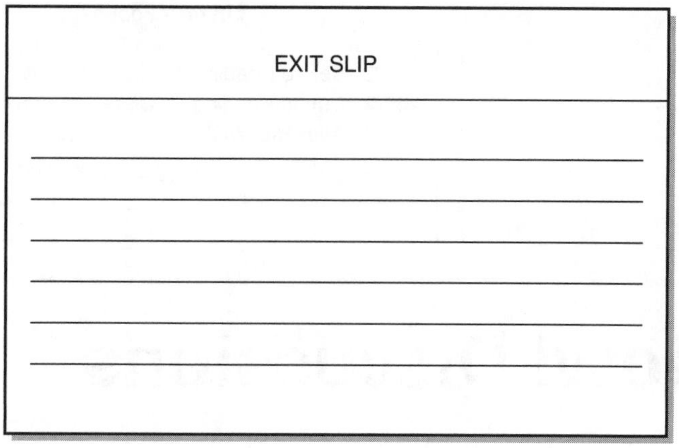

write. These students are very good at writing exit slips because all of their teachers use them regularly. For example, Javier wrote the following for this exit slip from PE:

> I was on my game today. That warmup was good and the team played good. I need to do cardio tonight, but right now I'm stoked that we were able to play and get along. We won, but that didn't matter too much. Getting along as the team matters more.

9

Fishbowl Discussions

Class discussions should involve all students, not just those who are vocal and always likely to respond, and they should result in more student–student interaction patterns rather than student–teacher patterns (Alvermann, O'Brien, & Dillon, 1990). Therefore, the best discussion strategies are those that enrich understanding of disciplinary topics through the exchange of multiple viewpoints and enlist the participation of virtually every student (Larson, 1999). One such strategy is the fishbowl discussion (Green, 2000). This strategy is well labeled because it involves one group of students looking in on another smaller group of students in a manner not unlike watching fish through the clear glass of an aquarium. The small group carries on a conversation about the issue or topic while the outside group listens and prepares questions and comments for the discussants. These roles are frequently rotated to ensure all students play an active part in discussing, listening, and questioning.

STEP-BY-STEP

1. Identify a focus for class discussion. Typically, the more controversial and charged the issue, the greater the level of engagement on the part of students. Thus, a topic in science such as the water cycle for students living in arid and semiarid parts of the country might be considered from an environmental perspective resulting in the following issue: *The region needs to increase the volume of potable water in order to develop and expand. How can this be done without upsetting the current ecological balance?*

2. Ask students to turn to a neighbor and talk about their ideas and opinions related to the issue. Tell students to take notes on their discussion. Allow enough time for a reasonable exchange of ideas and viewpoints, which can be determined by moving around the room to monitor and facilitate.

3. Demonstrate the format and expectations of a fishbowl discussion. This is best accomplished in a "dry run" of the activity. Ask for four or five volunteers to sit around a table or a cluster of desks in the middle of the room. Have the other students gather in a circle.

4. Get the discussion started by telling the discussants sitting in a cluster to talk among themselves about the ideas and opinions they raised when conversing with a partner.

5. Tell the other students to listen carefully to their classmates while they engage in a small-group discussion and take notes or jot down questions to share afterward.

6. Allow the discussants to talk for 5 minutes or so, getting involved only if the discussion dies or to ensure everyone is contributing and taking turns.

7. When the small group finishes or is stopped, ask the other students to make comments on the discussion they observed and/or ask questions of the discussants. This is an ideal time to model appropriate comments and questions.
8. Gather another small group of volunteer discussants, and continue the fishbowl process until all students have had the opportunity to be inside the fishbowl and they are clear about their roles and expectations.

APPLICATION AND EXAMPLES

An English literature teacher began reconsidering his role as interrogator during a typical class discussion when he noticed it was causing most students to mentally retreat. In order to maximize participation, he began searching for an alternative discussion strategy that created a context for students to reflect, converse, share, and critique in an atmosphere of mutual respect. When he discovered and began using the fishbowl approach he soon found that it allowed students to plumb the depths of a topic by inviting them to explore and challenge their various points of view on the topic. It also stimulated critical thinking and engendered interest in and motivation for learning. And, perhaps most important, it demonstrated to his students that their input was desired and respected.

He set up a fishbowl discussion with his students around an issue in a scene from Shakespeare's *Hamlet* they had just read and viewed. He first organized a closed circle of five desks in the middle of the room, then randomly called on five students and asked them to sit in the specially arranged desks. He asked the remaining class members to gather around the group seated in the middle, then posed a question for that group: *What if Hamlet had not killed Polonius? Could he have saved himself from a certain life of tragedy? Please explain.* While the five students began proposing different possible outcomes of the play and offering rationales, the others were asked to watch and listen quietly. Some suggested the Danish prince might have left his homeland forever; others speculated he could have rallied an army against the treacherous king; still others were sure Hamlet's personality was so flawed he would have met a tragic end, regardless. At this point, the teacher elicited reactions to the small-group discussion from those students watching from the outside. This approach allows those students looking in on the discussion to critique and assess the ideas of the fishbowl discussants. The teacher then selected a new group of five students and asked them to discuss a new but related question.

References

Alvermann, D., O'Brien, D., & Dillon, D. (1990). What teachers do when they say they're having discussions of content area reading assignments: A qualitative analysis. *Reading Research Quarterly, 25*, 296–322.

Green, T. (2000). Responding and sharing: Techniques for energizing classroom discussions. *The Clearing House, 73*, 331–334.

Larson, B. (1999). Influence on social studies teachers' use of classroom discussion. *The Social Studies, 90*, 125–132.

10

Literacy Focus

⬭ Before Reading	⬭ Fluency
⬭ During Reading	⬛ Comprehension
⬛ After Reading	⬛ Vocabulary
	⬭ Writing
	⬭ Oral Language

Found Poems

Language has a powerful influence on learning concepts. Found poems (Hobgood, 1998) encourage students to discover how authors use specific words and images to capture the essence of their writing and the information they would like to convey to the reader. Found poems not only provide a scaffold for writing, but also focus students on vocabulary and key ideas from their content area reading. Basically, students use the author's words to create their own new text.

The key to writing useful found poetry is selecting an interesting piece of writing and carefully considering the author's purpose as demonstrated through word choice. Classroom compilations of found poems might be created from books that include a series of short passages related to a common theme or topic, such as *Guys Write for Guys Read,* Scieszka's (2005) edited collection of personal narratives, memoirs, and stories contributed by male authors; *Madam President* (Thimmesh, 2004), which provides snapshots of women who have made political history; or *Shake, Rattle & Roll: The Founders of Rock & Roll* (George-Warren, 2001), which includes one-page descriptions of famous musicians. Primary sources such as speeches (e.g., Dr. King's "I Have a Dream" or interviews (e.g., *Oh Freedom! Kids Talk about the Civil Rights Movement with the People Who Made It Happen,* King & Osborne, 1997) can also be examined more carefully by "finding" a poem within them. In addition, critical scenes in novels often include powerful language that reflects the prominent themes or features of the book.

STEP-BY-STEP

When having students find poems in their reading, it is crucial to emphasize purposeful reading first. Otherwise, students may focus on the technical aspects of creating a poem while ignoring meaning. The following steps in developing a found poem should follow a careful reading of the text:

1. Circle or list the strongest words in the passage. Pay special attention to powerful verbs, significant nouns, and well-chosen adjectives. Strike through any words that are repetitive or unnecessary.
2. Start the poem with a strong word or phrase. As much as possible, honor the author's original order of words. Think about which phrases require emphasis, and consider line breaks accordingly. Strong words and phrases should stand alone.
3. Edit the poem for verb tense. If you add words to maintain grammatical sense, keep them to a minimum.
4. Title the poem and write a final draft. Be sure to add a complete citation for the text you used.

Students' own freewriting and journal entries are also excellent sources for found poetry. This is particularly true for students whose technical expertise in writing does not match their knowledge and experiences. A rough, unedited piece of writing often masks deep thinking. Highlighting short and compelling sections of the text helps students clarify their expression of ideas.

APPLICATION AND EXAMPLES

For instance, one student "found" the following poem in a section of *We Are Americans: Voices of the Immigrant Experience* (Hoobler & Hoobler, 2003) that emphasizes the experiences of immigrant schoolchildren:

School and Immigrant Children in the early 1900s

Memorization, drill

Forced to desks, bolted

Talking forbidden

You ain't any good

Lice probes with two pencils

Humiliation

Teachers: critical

Mother: Don't smell.... Teach

Whereas the passage read by the student was several pages long, she was able to extract the most salient words and images from the text to create a short, compelling, and informative poem that summarized the text.

A student in a health class "found" a poem focused on the main character in *Cut* (McCormick, 2000), whose mental illness manifests itself in self-mutilation using the jagged edge of a pie pan. The original text read:

> I lay my index finger lightly on the edge of one half, testing it. It's rough and right. I bring the inside of my wrist up to meet it. A tingle crawls across my scalp. I close my eyes and wait. But nothing happens. There's no release. Just a weird tugging sensation. I open my eyes. The skin on my wrist is drawn up in a wrinkle, snagged on the edge. I pull it in the other direction and a dull throbbing starts in my wrist. I hold my breath and push down on the piece of metal. It sinks in neatly. A sudden liquid heat floods my body. The pain is so sharp, so sudden, I catch my breath. There's no rush, no relief. Just pain, a keen, pulsing pain. I drop the pie plate and grasp my wrist with my other hand, dimly aware even as I'm doing it that this is something I've never done before. Never tried to stop the blood. Never interfered. It's never hurt like this before. And it's never not worked. (pp. 50–51)

The student's poem read:

Testing the edge—my finger

Testing the edge—it's rough

Testing the edge—my wrist to meet it

I wait. I wait. I wait. Nothing.

I open my eyes.

Sudden liquid heat—stop the blood. Never, never, never, never not worked.

References

George-Warren, H. (2001). *Shake, rattle & roll: The founders of rock & roll.* Boston: Houghton Mifflin.

Hobgood, J. M. (1998). Found poetry. *Voices from the Middle, 5*(2), 30.

Hoobler, T., & Hoobler, D. (2003). *We are Americans: Voices of the immigrant experience.* New York: Scholastic.

King, C., & Osborne, L. B. (1997). *Oh freedom! Kids talk about the Civil Rights Movement with the people who made it happen.* New York: Knopf.

McCormick, P. (2000). *Cut.* New York: Scholastic.

Scieszka, J. (Ed.). (2005). *Guys write for guys read.* New York: Viking Press.

Thimmesh, C. (2004). *Madam president.* Boston: Houghton Mifflin.

11

Generative Reading

Although we know that active, generative reading and learning increases engagement and promotes long-term recall of newly learned information and ideas (Caccamise & Snyder, 2005; Grabowski, 1996), secondary classroom practices traditionally position students to assume roles of responder and reactor as opposed to initiator and generator (Mayer, 2002). Students become so conditioned to passive roles that they may only offer comments, present ideas, or provide answers when the teacher or textbook prompts them to do so. Helping youth become generators of their own reading and learning prompts (Wittrock, 1990) means changing the relationship between students and teachers and students and text. Teachers will need to position youth to inquire proactively into disciplinary topics and to initiate strategies for understanding instead of waiting to be told how and what to think (Pressley & Hilden, 2004; Ritchie & Volkl, 2000).

STEP-BY-STEP

Youth can be taught to be independent, generative readers and learners if that is a consistent expectation of them, and if they receive appropriate instructional support. Here is our recommendation for facilitating students' transition from passive or reactive learners to generators of their own learning aids.

1. Provide structured practice in which teacher and text prompts are converted into student-generated prompts. Notice in Figure 11.1 how every prompt or aid from the text and teacher can be generated by the learner.
2. Use a model-elicit approach in which a text-based prompt is generated by the teacher and then a similar prompt elicited from students. Curiously, in the name of crafting reader-friendly textbooks, publishers have so much scaffolding and so many aids built into disciplinary texts that it would seem there is little left for students to generate on their own. This trend toward packing in the support structures in textbooks has further contributed to student passivity.
3. Work with one or two prompts at a time to ensure students have sufficient experience with the generative process to develop expertise. For example, because headings and subheadings are perhaps the most abundant aids to organizing thinking about textbook information, these might be an ideal focus for initial generative work. After discussing how subheadings subsume the main points that follow, students can be asked to create their own subheadings for a section of text. Next might come modeling and eliciting question prompts.
4. Allow students to work in pairs to generate their reading and learning prompts. These can be shared with the entire class and critiqued for their usefulness for constructing and extracting meaning from text.

Figure 11.1 Teacher Text Prompts and Learner Generations

If the text or teacher provides . . .	Then the learner should be taught to:
Headings and subheadings	Compose headings and subheadings
Titles	Compose titles
Highlighted words or phrases	Highlight important words and phrases
Questions	Develop questions
Objectives	Write objectives
Summaries	Produce oral and/or written summaries
Marginal gloss	Create marginal gloss
Analogies	Give analogies
Descriptions or presentations of experiments	Describe or present experiments
Examples	Provide examples
Graphs and tables	Prepare graphs and tables
Maps	Draw maps
Problems to be solved	Create problems to be solved
Graphic overviews	Make graphic overviews

5. The goal is to wean students from a dependence on the teacher to model and elicit generative prompts and aids. After all, if students generate prompts for reading and learning only when requested by the teacher, then they have failed to move out of their passive learning roles.
6. Finally, take advantage of every opportunity to turn over responsibility for generating prompts while reading and learning to the students. For example, if the pattern has been to ask whole-class discussion questions interspersed throughout the reading of a story or novel, pause periodically and have students turn to a partner and generate their own discussion questions. Students can then ask questions of each other.

APPLICATION AND EXAMPLES

Once discovered, generative strategies become a permanent part of disciplinary teachers' instructional practices. The benefits were obvious right away for a science teacher who watched how enthusiastic her students became when they were asked to add their own experiments to the one presented in the textbook on gravity. She explained to the class that they needed to go one step beyond just reading about what others have done to demonstrate the effects of gravitational fields. She challenged them to design their own demonstrations of some principle of gravity using only the available materials in the science lab. Students worked in teams of three and were required to present their experiment to the rest of the class. The observers were to document the details of the experiment, paying particular attention to the results, and then propose an explanation. Their explanation would be compared with the experimenters'.

One team set up an experiment by first placing newspaper on the floor. They positioned a chair in the middle of the paper, and then two students lay on their stomachs on the newspaper on either side of the chair with their heads facing forward. Finally, the third student stood on the chair with her arms outstretched holding an orange in each hand. The rest of the class gathered around curious about what would happen next. The student on the chair dropped both oranges at the same time so that they would fall right in front of her prostrate partners. The two immediately called in unison "now" to signal when the oranges hit the newspaper. Then the procedure was repeated, but this time an orange and a grape were dropped together. Again, the two students on the floor yelled "now" at exactly the same time. Eventually, the students observing the experiment explained the phenomenon as the universal law of gravity in which the force is equal on all matter regardless of its mass.

By generating experiments that applied principles of gravity instead of merely reading about an experiment in their textbooks, the science students were much more engaged in the knowledge construction process.

References

Caccamise, D., & Snyder, L. (2005). Theory and pedagogical practices of text comprehension. *Topics in Language Disorders, 25,* 5–20.

Grabowski, B. L. (1996). Generative learning: Past, present and future. In D. H. Jonassen (Ed.), *Handbook of research for educational communications and technology* (pp. 897–918). New York: Macmillan Library.

Mayer, R. E. (2002). Rote versus meaningful learning. *Theory Into Practice, 41,* 226–233.

Pressley, M., & Hilden, K. (2004). Toward more ambitious comprehension instruction. In E. Silliman & L. Wilkinson (Eds.), *Language and literacy learning in schools* (pp. 151–174). New York: Guilford Press.

Ritchie, D., & Volkl, C. (2000). Effectiveness of two generative learning strategies in the science classroom. *School Science & Mathematics, 100*(2), 83–90.

Wittrock, M. (1990). Generative processes of comprehension. *Educational Psychologist, 24,* 345–376.

12

Literacy Focus

⬤ Before Reading	⬭ Fluency
⬭ During Reading	⬤ Comprehension
⬭ After Reading	⬤ Vocabulary
	⬭ Writing
	⬭ Oral Language

Guest Speakers

How often have we heard the lament of the teenager: "When am I ever going to need this?" Many educators are familiar with the benefits of experiential learning (Dewey 1938). These experiences are especially beneficial to adolescents who are looking for the relevance of their school studies. The application of academic knowledge to real-world situations can be transformative in the lives of our students. Indeed, nearly all secondary schools in the country offer internships and community service opportunities as part of the curriculum. Kolb (1984) noted that these experiences help students appreciate that knowledge is constantly evolving, not fixed and static.

However, many of us do not have the ability to create experiences for our students outside the classroom. Guest speakers can serve as a way to invite the world in, while making connections to the topics of study. The application of mathematics in the world is made clear by a visit from an engineer or designer. Visiting performance and visual artists can share their craft with budding dancers and painters. History teachers have long known that guest speakers can make history come alive. Their use has been documented in studies of classroom visits by Holocaust survivors (Glanz, 1999), Vietnam War veterans (Poling, 2000), and recent immigrants to the United States (Giannangelo & Bolding, 1998). A study of 601 middle school students found that contact with people in science fields was predictive of their interest in science careers, especially for girls (Koszalka, Grabowski, & Darling, 2005).

STEP-BY-STEP

1. A successful visit by a speaker begins with careful planning with the guest. Be sure to provide the speaker with details about the size, age, and background knowledge of the audience—your students. Many guest speakers are not educators and are unfamiliar with the developmental needs of young learners. Therefore, put your information in writing so he or she can refer to it later. Other useful details include procedures for parking, signing in, and finding the classroom. Be sure to provide time boundaries as well. Those who have been away from schools may forget that the bell system trumps everything else. Find out what technology needs your speaker will require so that you can arrange for this equipment in advance.

2. Like your guest speaker, your students need to be prepared as well. Some students view visits by guests with the same regard as a substitute teacher—in other words, this doesn't really "count." In the days and weeks before his or her arrival, refer to the speaker and the information that will be shared. Discuss the background and expertise of the speaker and share examples of work the person has done, if appropriate. The day before the guest arrives, we require our students to prepare a list of questions in advance (see Figure 12.1). We discuss the factors that make a question interesting, and

Figure 12.1 Student Form for Guest Speakers

Name of Speaker _____ Date _____	
Purpose of Visit	
Unique Experiences	
Connections	

Questions	Answers

Source: From *Improving Adolescent Literacy: Strategies That Work,* by D. Fisher and N. Frey, 2003, Upper Saddle River, NJ: Merrill/Prentice Hall. Reprinted by permission.

remind them of the etiquette of welcoming guests into our class. They are accountable for their notes, and we collect them after the guest speaker's appearance for grading. We also let them know that information shared by the guest speaker will appear on chapter and unit tests.

3. When the big day arrives, have the room and students organized in advance. No guest wants to feel as though he or she has interrupted the class. Desks and students should be arranged in anticipation of the arrival. Remember to notify the office about your guest as well. This will make for a smooth introduction to the school.

4. Guest speakers provide a great opportunity to model engaged learning. Don't treat this class period as time off for you. Few things are more insulting to a guest than the sight of the teacher grading papers or answering e-mails. Ask questions of your guest and make connections for your students to other topics they have been studying. Let your students see you as an active, lifelong learner.

5. Remember to follow up the visit with a note of thanks to your speaker. These are truly appreciated—have you noticed how often these are displayed in places of business? If the guest speaker's topic was related to his or her work, copy the letter to the employer as well.

6. You know what they say about the best laid plans. Emergencies do happen, so it is wise to have an alternative plan at the ready.

APPLICATION AND EXAMPLES

Ms. Webster's earth science class has been studying the formation of galaxies in the universe for several weeks, and is now preparing for a guest speaker—an astronomer from the local planetarium. She has been in communication with Dr. Hayes for several weeks, and has sent her detailed information regarding the class and their studies. Dr. Lee was particularly appreciative to receive a photocopy of the chapters they had been reading, as well as a list of Websites utilized in a recent WebQuest conducted at the beginning of the unit. Because her visit will be during the day, she has prepared her visit to include a solar observation.

The science teacher has also been busy readying her students for the guest speaker. Because she and Dr. Lee had communicated about the topic in advance, Ms. Webster has incorporated aspects of this into her class discussions. The class has conducted research on the topic and has prepared questions to ask of Dr. Lee.

When the day of the visit arrives, Dr. Lee finds herself being welcomed in the front office by two of Ms. Webster's students. She has sent them to help Dr. Lee carry the equipment, and to escort her to the classroom. She arrives to a room full of students who have questions at the ready. Ms. Webster has given each student a nametag to wear so the guest can address them by name.

After a 15-minute discussion, Ms. Webster and Dr. Lee lead the students outside for the solar observation. Because the students have been prepared, they already know the dangers of observing the sun without proper protection. Dr. Lee has brought several refracting telescopes featuring wedge diagonal apertures designed for solar observation. Because she and Ms. Webster communicated in the weeks before the visit, Dr. Lee knew she would need several telescopes in order to give each student time to view the sun during the allotted time.

After returning to their classroom, the students asked more questions, including many directed at her own schooling and experiences as an astronomer. As the end of the class period approached, Ms. Webster thanked the guest speaker, who was treated to a warm round of applause. Both the science teacher and the astronomer remarked later that it was a highlight of their year.

References

Dewey, J. (1938). *Experience and education.* Chicago: Free Press.

Giannangelo, D. M., & Bolding, R. A. (1998). Ethnocentrism, geography, and foreign guest speakers: An attempt to change attitudes. *Journal of Middle States Council for the Social Studies,* 122–126.

Glanz, J. (1999). Ten suggestions for teaching the Holocaust. *History Teacher, 32,* 547–565.

Kolb, D. (1984). *Experiential learning: Experience as the source of learning and development.* Upper Saddle River, NJ: Prentice Hall.

Koszalka, T. A., Grabowski, B. L., & Darling, N. (2005). Predictive relationships between web and human resource use and middle school students' interest in science careers: An exploratory analysis. *Journal of Career Development, 31,* 171–184.

Poling, L. G. (2000). The real world: Community speakers in the classroom. *Social Education, 64*(4), 8–10.

13

Literacy Focus

- ⬭ Before Reading
- ⬭ During Reading
- ⬛ After Reading

- ⬭ Fluency
- ⬛ Comprehension
- ⬛ Vocabulary
- ⬭ Writing
- ⬭ Oral Language

Independent Reading

There are good reasons to believe that time spent in engaged reading is an important instructional priority. It is powerfully linked to differences in reading achievement (Allington, 2001) and in vocabulary development (Nagy, Anderson, & Herman, 1987). Schools that maintain regular reading times see positive differences in schoolwide reading scores (Fisher, 2004). Plus, independent reading may have benefits that extend beyond the official curriculum. For instance, students who participate in classroom reading programs in school are more likely to read outside school (Pilgreen & Krashen, 1993); this is particularly important knowing that voluntary reading outside school is closely tied to reading and writing competence (Anderson, Wilson, & Fielding, 1988). Students also report that the opportunity to just read is actually their most preferred literacy-related activity, and that when teachers set aside time for them to spend alone with text, they are more likely to think and learn (Ivey & Broaddus, 2001).

STEP-BY-STEP

Although opportunities for independent reading have been limited mainly to English classrooms and schoolwide reading programs, it stands to reason that these benefits—deep thinking about a subject and more voluntary reading—should also apply to content area classrooms. Furthermore, in a case in which seventh-grade students were given a choice—during a daily self-selected reading time—between reading anything they wanted or reading from a selection of diverse, multilevel trade books related to the life science topics they were studying, most students selected science reading (Ivey & Broaddus, 2003). Other widely embraced and research-based instructional frameworks, such as concept-oriented reading instruction (Guthrie et al., 1996), emphasize time spent with text as an important curricular component.

APPLICATION AND EXAMPLES

The key to successful independent reading times in content classrooms—whether through wide, self-selected reading in the subject to increase interest and knowledge or through specific inquiry projects—is offering readable, engaging texts and providing support for individual students who have not yet adopted the habit of reading on their own. When students are reading on their own during content area classes, the teacher's instructional role is not to keep everyone on task, per se, but instead to facilitate engagement. Just telling students to read or concentrate does not address what students need. Some students who do not yet read with confidence will need help getting started and maintaining independent reading (Ivey, 2002). While most students are engaged in silent reading, teachers can take the opportunity to support those who need help. There are three potential ways that teachers might facilitate struggling readers' engagement with independent reading, keeping in mind that the purpose is to enhance the experience rather than interrupt it (Worthy, Broaddus, & Ivey, 2001):

Help students find materials they can read and want to read. Inexperienced readers do not always select the books that make sense to them, so they will not become engaged in reading and may appear noncompliant during reading times. But Bomer (1999) talks about the need for teachers to have a better understanding about book selection: "When I am reading in bed before I go to sleep and I suddenly realize that the last page and a half of print has not affected my thought at all, I notice, and turn out the light. Struggling readers don't notice—to them, everything seems fine, because that barrenness of meaning is what they're used to" (p. 27).

Content area teachers can actually teach students about reading that makes sense through conversations about book selection. For instance, while other students read self-selected books about the experiences of children in World War II, Renita sat in front of her choice seemingly uninterested in reading. In a quick conversation with Renita, her teacher found that she had haphazardly selected a difficult historical fiction novel. Her teacher then located a stack of easier, but interesting books that spanned a range of formats and genres, and she read short excerpts to Renita and urged her to think about which text appealed to her most. Renita quickly chose *The Orphans of Normandy* (Amis, 2003), which uses children's actual drawings and captions to tell the story of a hundred schoolgirls who escaped an Allied invasion. She was engaged in reading for the rest of the class period.

Get students started in the texts they have selected. For example, noticing that Cody was looking around the room as other students self-selected biographies, his English teacher offered to read alternating pages of *The Champ: The Story of Muhammad Ali* (Bolden, 2004), stopping to share his own reactions as he read. For instance, when they learned that as a child, Cassius Clay, as he was then called, "developed a curious love for dodging rocks" (p. 4), the teacher commented, "That explains why he was so good at dodging punches in the boxing ring." This modeling of curiosity and response inspired Cody to keep reading when the teacher walked away.

Help individual students overcome dilemmas as they arise in their reading. For example, eighth-grader Shawn's science teacher sat with him as he read *The Bug Scientists* (Jackson, 2002). When he got to the word *carcasses,* Shawn was able to pronounce it correctly, but he asked his teacher what it meant. The teacher took this opportunity to explain to Shawn that sometimes you can figure out a word's meaning from the other words, phrases, and sentences around it. He reread the passage containing carcasses: "[Insects] help keep the earth clean by eating dead animals. Otherwise the roads would be littered with carcasses" (p. 10). Shawn then guessed that a carcass was a dead animal. This discussion addressed Shawn's immediate confusion, and it also gave him some ideas for how to tackle similar dilemmas when the teacher is not around.

References

Allington, R. L. (2001). *What really matters for struggling readers: Designing research-based programs.* New York: Longman.

Anderson, R. C., Wilson, P. T., & Fielding, L. G. (1988). Growth in reading and how children spend their time outside school. *Reading Research Quarterly, 23*, 285–303.

Amis, N. (2003). *The orphans of Normandy: A true story of World War II told through drawings by children.* New York: Atheneum.

Bomer, R. B. (1999). Conferring with struggling readers: The test of our craft, courage, and hope. *The New Advocate, 12*(1), 21–38.

Bolden, T. (2004). *The champ: The story of Muhammad Ali.* New York: Knopf.

Fisher, D. (2004). Setting the "opportunity to read" standard: Resuscitating the SSR program in an urban high school. *Journal of Adolescent & Adult Literacy, 48*, 138–150.

Guthrie, J. T. et al. (1996). Growth of literacy engagement: Changes in motivations and strategies during concept-oriented reading instruction. *Reading Research Quarterly, 31*, 306–332.

Ivey, G. (2002). Making reading time count for middle school students. *California Reader, 36*, 31–35.

Ivey, G., & Broaddus, K. (2001). "Just plain reading": A survey of what makes students want to read in middle school classrooms. *Reading Research Quarterly, 36*, 350–377.

Ivey, G., & Broaddus, K. (2003, December). *"It's good to read if you can read it": What matters to middle school students in content area independent reading.* Paper presented at the National Reading Conference, Scottsdale, AZ.

Jackson, D. M. (2002). *The bug scientists.* Boston: Houghton Mifflin.

Nagy, W., Anderson, R. C., & Herman, P. A. (1987). Learning word meanings from context during normal reading. *American Educational Research Journal, 24*, 237–270.

Pilgreen, J., & Krashen, S. (1993). Sustained silent reading with English as a second language high school students: Impact on comprehension, reading frequency, and reading enjoyment. *School Library Media Quarterly, 22*, 21–23.

Worthy, J., Broaddus, K., & Ivey, G. (2001). *Pathways to independence: Reading, writing, and learning in grades 3–8.* New York: Guilford Press.

14

Literacy Focus

━━ Before Reading ⬭ Fluency
⬭ During Reading ━━ Comprehension
⬭ After Reading ⬭ Vocabulary
⬭ Writing
⬭ Oral Language

Interest Surveys, Questionnaires, and Interviews

Surveys in research have been used in productive ways to help educators understand the literacy-related needs of adolescents. For instance, Worthy, Moorman, and Turner (1999) learned much about the reading preferences of sixth graders from a study reported in a paper appropriately titled *What Johnny Likes to Read Is Hard to Find in School.* Similarly, Ivey and Broaddus (2001) asked over 1,700 middle schoolers what motivated them to read in their language arts classes. Their top responses included having time to read in school, interesting reading materials, and opportunities for their teacher to read aloud to them.

But surveys and questionnaires can also be useful at the classroom level when they are administered by teachers to design instruction for particular contexts and specific groups of students. Gathering information from students in content area classes is especially enlightening. Oftentimes, we learn that even students who appear to be failing the school curriculum are actually interested in school-related topics (e.g., World War II, weather, poetry), but this knowledge is frequently masked by reading and writing activities that may be too difficult. Surveys and questionnaires may actually help us identify the literacy-based learning experiences that highlight or capitalize on students' interests rather than hide them. When students can tell us what they prefer to read and write, what kinds of literacy experiences are most useful to them, and what kinds of support they need to read and write more productively, we are in a better position to provide truly responsive instruction. For instance, if a student tells us they have *never* had a good reading experience in English class, it stands to reason that more of the same kinds of texts and instruction they have received previously will not likely lead to motivated, purposeful reading.

STEP-BY-STEP

One important way to gather information from students is to survey the genres and formats of books the students most prefer to read. Figure 14.1 includes a checklist that could be given to a whole class during the first week of school to get a general idea of student preferences. The key to interpreting the results of checklist surveys is not necessarily to just calculate percentages of response across students to measure the most popular materials, but instead to look at the range of individual interests. For instance, whereas a large percentage of a class may report interest in series books, it is no less important to pay attention to a small group of students who appreciate picture books or historical fic-

Figure 14.1 Reading Preferences Checklist

1. _____ Adventure novels		11. _____ Series books	
2. _____ Funny novels		12. _____ Books or magazines about sports	
3. _____ Fiction novels about people my age		13. _____ Magazines about people	
4. _____ Fantasy and science fiction novels		14. _____ Biographies	
5. _____ Scary books		15. _____ Magazines about hobbies	
6. _____ Historical fiction		16. _____ Magazines about cars and trucks	
7. _____ Information books about science		17. _____ Books about animals	
8. _____ Information books about history		18. _____ Picture books	
9. _____ Information books about math		19. _____ Poetry books	
10. _____ Books written mostly for adults		20. _____ Cartoons, comics, or graphic novels	

Figure 14.2 Sample Questions that Elicit Information About Students' Reading and Writing

- Tell me about yourself as a reader/writer.
- If you could read anything, what would it be? Why?
- What makes a person a good reader/writer?
- What makes you want to read in (name of subject area)?
- Tell me about a time when you got hooked on a book.
- Tell me about a good experience you had with reading in (name of subject).
- Tell me about a bad experience you had with a book.
- Tell me about a bad experience you had with reading in (name of subject).
- Tell me about a time when you got hooked on something you were writing.
- What about writing in (name of subject)?
- Tell me about a bad experience with writing.
- What about writing in (name of subject)?
- How do you choose the books you read?
- How do you decide whether or not to read a book?
- Tell me about the reading you do in school.
- Tell me about the reading you do outside of school.
- Tell me what teachers have done that helps you the most with reading.
- What advice would you give to someone who does not want to read?
- If you could change anything about yourself as a reader, what would it be?

tion. The intent behind getting information from all students is to be able to respond to individual needs.

To get a more specific notion of students' reading and writing needs, interviews or open-ended responses may be in order. Figure 14.2 includes a list of questions that elicit rich responses about students' literacy experiences. Notice that all of these questions allow for elaborate responses rather than a yes/no response. Also, it helps to ask about specific experiences with reading and writing. Detailing a particular literacy activity or text that was especially meaningful is much more useful than giving a general response of when reading and writing work for students.

APPLICATION AND EXAMPLES

Interest surveys, questionnaires, and interviews of all types are regularly used by teachers who want to meet individual student needs. For example, in her physics class, Ms. Greene uses an interest survey to create "expert groups" in which students delve deeper into topics and then share their learnings with the class. In his English class, Mr. Mongure uses a questionnaire to identify books for his students to read. He does not use a "whole-class novel" but rather identifies books that contain the literary devices he is teaching—books that are written about the topics his students want to know more about.

References

Ivey, G., & Broaddus, K. (2001). "Just plain reading": A survey of what makes students want to read in middle school classrooms. *Reading Research Quarterly, 36*, 350–377.

Worthy, J., Moorman, M., & Turner, M. (1999). What Johnny likes to read is hard to find in school. *Reading Research Quarterly, 34*, 12–27.

15

Literacy Focus

⬭ Before Reading   ⬭ Fluency
⬛ During Reading   ⬛ Comprehension
⬭ After Reading   ⬭ Vocabulary
                          ⬭ Writing
                          ⬭ Oral Language

Jigsaw

As content teachers, we want our students to understand that knowledge is not fixed and static, and that new information shapes our current understandings of the biological, social, and physical world. This means that we incorporate additional source materials into our curriculum to broaden our students' exposure to written text. History teachers use primary source documents to foster document-based questioning (Stovel, 2000). Art teachers require students to view a wide range of works of art to understand cultural influences and aesthetic principles (Efland, 2004). However, the logistics of introducing worthwhile written materials into a classroom and providing students with quality time to read and discuss them can be challenging. A jigsaw method of collaborative reading and discussion can solve some of these issues.

Jigsaw was first developed by Aronson (1978, 2000) to promote social and cooperative development among diverse groups of students. His initial intention had less to do with learning content than with breaking down barriers between students in a recently desegregated elementary school in Texas. Before long, teachers and researchers discovered that students were reaching more sophisticated levels of understanding about the content, as well as the material. Studies indicating deeper levels of student learning have been conducted in such diverse content areas as atomic structures in middle school chemistry (Eilks, 2005), complex numbers in intermediate algebra (Lucas, 2000), and Thoreau in high school English (Kohleffel, 1996).

The selection of the texts to be read can vary depending on the intended purpose. The readings may all be closely related to one another (complementary), or they may offer different points of view on the same topic (conflicting) (Hartman & Allison, 1996). A third approach divides a single reading into sections, so that it can be fully understood only when each group member has had the opportunity to discuss his or her portion of the reading (Aronson, 1978).

STEP-BY-STEP

A jigsaw lesson requires that each student be a member of two groups—a *home group* and an *expert group*. Students begin and end the activity in a home group. The students in this group are responsible for teaching one another each aspect of the reading. Students then travel to an expert group. The members of the group read and discuss the same text, or portion of the text. They question and clarify their understanding until they are comfortable with the content of the reading. Students return to their home group to listen to each member explain their reading, and to teach their own. A procedural map for grouping students in a jigsaw activity appears in Figure 15.1.

Divide students into heterogeneous groups and distribute reading materials. We recommend that groups be no larger than four or five students, as the discussion portion is often

Figure 15.1 Jigsaw Procedure

Phase One: Home Groups

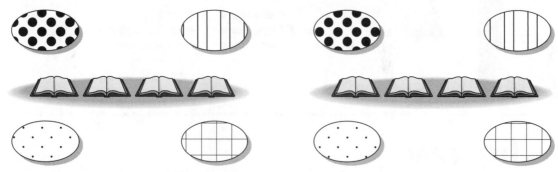

Students meet in home groups to divide the readings among themselves.

Phase Two: Expert Groups

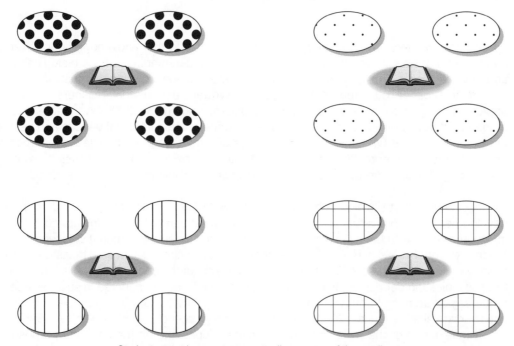

Students meet in expert groups to discuss one of the readings.

Phase Three: Home Groups

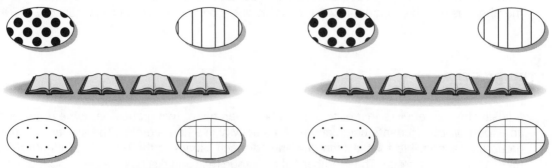

Students reconvene in expert groups to discuss all of the readings.

Source: From *Language Arts Workshop: Purposeful Reading and Writing Instruction,* by N. Frey and D. Fisher, 2006, Upper Saddle River, NJ: Merrill/Prentice Hall. Used with permission.

rushed in larger groups. Review the jigsaw procedure with them in advance of the activity. We find that displaying a schedule with times is useful.

1. Provide a brief overview of each reading, or portion of the reading if you are using a single piece of text. Give students a few minutes to determine who will be responsible for each assigned reading.
2. Remind students that the desired outcome is for each member of the class to understand all of the readings. Because no one is reading every text, it is incumbent upon the members of the expert group to understand their assigned reading well, and to be able to present it effectively to others. As well, each student in the home group is responsible for listening carefully to each speaker and taking notes as needed.
3. Instruct students to go to their expert groups to read and discuss a common piece of text. This part of the activity involves an extended period of silent reading, followed by discussion, therefore it is helpful to physically separate the groups. Consider labeling areas of the classroom with a number or name of the reading to minimize lost time in transition.
4. After the expert groups have finished reading their assigned text, provide time for the group members to discuss and clarify their understanding of the content. Their meeting should end with a plan to summarize the text for their home groups. Encourage groups to highlight key information (if possible) or to make notes to speak from.
5. After the expert groups have finished their tasks, invite students to return to their home groups. Each member returning to the home group will now be an expert on one text. Direct them to discuss each text, marking time with a signal to keep a discussion from dragging on too long at the expense of another student. Remind students to take notes about key concepts, and to make connections as they learn about the other pieces of text.

APPLICATION AND EXAMPLES

Art history teacher Ms. Velasquez is introducing a unit on how death is represented in art from around the world. She has decided to provide a large photograph of each piece, accompanied by text explaining its origin, significance, and information about the artist. She has selected four works for her students to examine today. The first is a French fresco from 1355 called *The Black Death*. The informational text accompanying the photograph provides an overview of the bubonic plague, as well as a discussion of the use of arrows in Christian iconography as a representation of this disease. The second is a photograph of a Hemba death mask representing a chimpanzee, or So'o. In this African tribe, the chimpanzee represents death but also transforms into a clown figure, appearing in funeral processions to disrupt the mourning and cause people to dance instead. The third is a photograph of the city taken soon after the A-bomb was dropped on Hiroshima, Japan, in August 1945. The accompanying text explained the historical circumstances of the event, and asks the students to consider why the photographer would choose to represent the event through a photograph of the damage to structures, rather than the human toll. The fourth photograph was taken in modern-day Oaxaca, Mexico, on the Day of the Dead *(Dia de las Muertos)*. A large family is gathered around a colorful altar constructed in their home to honor the memory of a loved one.

Ms. Velasquez introduces the jigsaw lesson to students by first dividing them into groups of 4. Since she has 32 students in her class, there will be two expert groups for each artwork. She explains the task and previews each work, then asks the students to determine which artwork they will be responsible for. They quickly move to their expert groups, which have been denoted by a sign bearing a photocopy of the work of art.

As students examine the art and read the accompanying text, Ms. Velasquez circulates among the groups, providing guidance and asking questions of the members. After 15 minutes of lively discussion, they return to their home groups to share their works of art.

The home groups now reconvene and students take turns displaying the artwork and sharing information about it. They make observations about how death is viewed in each of these places and times. After all the members have shared their work of art, the conversation moves to deeper analysis across the pieces. One by one, the groups reach the conclusion that the cause of death seems to affect how it is represented. The plague of the 14th century and the bomb blast in Japan were catastrophic events that provoked artistic representations that were disturbing. The African and Mexican examples came from ceremonies involving death as a part of life. These artistic representations seemed to have the mourners in mind as they encouraged those still living to resume their lives and remember the dead with fondness and humor.

"These students seem to reach a level of critical thinking that I can't get to through lecture alone," commented Ms. Velasquez. "When I give them the space and time to discuss important ideas, it's truly amazing what they'll come up with."

References

Aronson, E. (1978). *The jigsaw classroom*. Beverly Hills, CA: Sage.

Aronson, E. (2000). *Nobody left to hate: Teaching compassion after Columbine*. New York: W. H. Freeman.

Efland, A. D. (2004). The entwined nature of the aesthetic: A discourse on visual culture. *Studies in Art Education, 45,* 234–251.

Eilks, I. (2005). Experiences and reflections about teaching atomic structure in a jigsaw classroom in lower secondary school chemistry lessons. *Journal of Chemical Education, 82,* 313–319.

Hartman, D. K., & Allison, J. (1996). Promoting inquiry-oriented discussions using multiple texts. In L. B. Gambrell & J. F. Almasi (Eds.), *Lively discussions! Fostering engaged readings* (pp. 106–133). Newark, DE: International Reading Association.

Kohleffel, R. (1996). Docendo discimus: Understanding H. D. Thoreau's *Walden* using the jigsaw reading technique. *Journal of Adolescent & Adult Literacy, 39,* 650–653.

Lucas, C. A. (2000). Jigsaw lesson for operations of complex numbers. *Primus, 10,* 219-224.

Stovel, J. E. (2000). Document analysis as a tool to strengthen student writing. *History Teacher, 33,* 501–509.

16

Literacy Focus

▬ Before Reading   ▭ Fluency
▭ During Reading   ▬ Comprehension
▭ After Reading   ▬ Vocabulary
                ▭ Writing
                ▭ Oral Language

KWL

KWL stands for "What do you *know?* What do you *want* to know? And what have you *learned?*" (Ogle, 1986). This discussion organizer mirrors the process of scientific inquiry inherent in any investigation. Typically, a teacher will arrange these questions into three columns and then prompt discussion about the next topic of study (see Figure 16.1). Student responses are recorded and then become the guide for subsequent study. KWL has been subsequently modified in a number of ways including KWL-Plus (Carr & Ogle, 1987), which adds summarization, and KWHL (Wills, 1995), which adds "*How* do we know?" to focus on sources of evidence. The recursive nature of inquiry is emphasized through KWLQ (Schmidt, 1999) when a fourth column for further questions is added at the end of the unit of study.

STEP-BY-STEP

Teachers across content area subjects have confirmed the usefulness and flexibility of the KWL technique for introducing a unit of study. Buehl (2001) identifies it as one of the instructional strategies essential in the repertoire of every secondary content area educator.

Figure 16.1 KWL Chart

What do I *know?*	What do I *want* to know?	What have I *learned?*

1. The first step is to identify the topic under investigation. This can be at the unit level (such as "biomes") or focused on specific topics (such as "plant cells" or "causes of World War I").
2. Introduce students to the topic. This can be done via a related read aloud, a class discussion, video/DVD, or other informational source. This step ensures that every student has some ideas about the topic under discussion.
3. Invite students to share what they already know about the topic. Record their responses, right or wrong, on the chart or board.
4. Ask students what they would like to know about the topic and record these responses in the appropriate column.
5. As the topic of study comes to a close, return to the KWL chart and ask students to review their initial knowledge and questions. Then invite discussion about what they have learned from their studies.
6. There are a number of variations for KWL as noted on page 47. You can use the "plus" to provide students an opportunity to summarize what they have learned, an "H" to engage students in a conversation about "*How* do we know?" or a "Q" for further questions.

APPLICATION AND EXAMPLES

Mike Jackson's students are required to conduct in-class research every 2 weeks on a historical figure of their choice. Mr. Jackson introduces research methods early in the year and models the first project on a single historical figure. He shows his students a selection of books, newspaper articles, Websites, and such featuring the person's work and invites questions. Subsequent research projects are student directed and encompass every era from medieval to present day. KWL charts are the initial component of any inquiry, and are expected with every research report. Recently, Anthony researched the life and work of Franklin D. Roosevelt (we've included grammar irregularities). His KWL chart is shown in Figure 16.2.

Mr. Jackson uses a 5-point rubric to guide the development of the KWL. The rubric is intended to guide the research process and includes the written report that is submitted (see Figure 16.3). Anthony received a "4" on his FDR paper.

Figure 16.2 Student's KWL for Franklin D. Roosevelt

What do I **know**?	What do I **want** to know?	What have I **learned**?
He was a president	When was he born?	Born in 1882 at Hyde Park, New York
He was famous	Where was he born?	
He's dead		
Married Eleanor	How long was he president?	Four terms
	When did he die?	April 12, 1945, in Warm Springs, Georgia
	What influenced him?	Unemployment and he wanted to be a good neighbor
	What did he do before he was president?	Law school, senator
	Was he in the military?	No, got polio when he was 39
		Said "the only thing we have to fear is fear itself."
		Made promise in 100 days U.S. would be better
		Made the "new deal"
		Let the government regulate the economy

Figure 16.3 KWL Grading Rubric

KWL Research Project Grading Rubric
K = What You Know   W = What You Want to Know   L = What You Learned

5. Exemplary!
✓ Completes the KWL chart with 7+ entries in each column.
✓ Demonstrates mastery in his/her writing skills, with little or no grammar and punctuation errors.
✓ Answers all of the W questions in the L section and includes all of the information in the writing assignment.
✓ Adds additional information in the writing section that was not part of the W section.

4. Exceeds Standards
✓ Completes the KWL chart with 5–6 entries in each column.
✓ Demonstrates above average writing skills in grammar and punctuation (errors do not interfere with meaning).
✓ Answers all of the W questions in the L section and includes all of the information in the written assignment.
✓ No new information.

3. Meets Standards
✓ Completes the KWL chart with 3–4 entries in each column.
✓ Demonstrates adequate writing skills in grammar and punctuation (some errors interfere with meaning).
✓ Answers more than half of the W questions in the L section and includes the information in the writing assignment.

2. Progressing
✓ Partially completed KWL chart.
✓ Answers less than half the W questions in the L section and includes the information in the writing assignment.

1. No Evidence
✓ Does not turn in a project for grading.
✓ Does not make an attempt at the project.

Source: Adapted from *Improving Adolescent Literacy: Strategies at Work,* by D. Fisher and N. Frey, 2004, Upper Saddle River, NJ: Merrill/Prentice Hall. Used with permission.

REFERENCES

Buehl, D. (2001). *Classroom strategies for interactive learning* (2nd ed.). Newark, DE: International Reading Association.

Carr, E., & Ogle, D. (1987). K-W-L plus: A strategy for comprehension and summarization. *Journal of Reading, 30,* 626–631.

Ogle, D. (1986). K-W-L: A teaching model that develops active reading of expository text. *The Reading Teacher, 39,* 564–570.

Schmidt, P. R. (1999). KWLQ: Inquiry and literacy learning in science. *The Reading Teacher, 52,* 789–792.

Wills, C. (1995). Voice of inquiry: Possibilities and perspectives. *Childhood Education, 71,* 261–265.

17

Literacy Focus

- Before Reading
- During Reading
- **After Reading**

- Fluency
- Comprehension
- **Vocabulary**
- **Writing**
- Oral Language

Language Experience Approach

Language experience approach (LEA) is an instructional approach first developed in the 1960s by Ashton-Warner (1963) to meet the needs of students who were struggling with conventional print. In a typical LEA lesson, the student talks while the teacher takes dictation. Once the message has been written down, the student should be able to read back the message. The goal of LEA is to facilitate speech-to-print connections for students. The written text becomes the instructional material the teacher can use because the student is familiar with both the content and context of the message.

LEA has been used with both young and old students, including adolescents identified as struggling readers and writers (Fisher & Frey, 2003). In addition, Brehaut (1994) demonstrated the use of LEA with an "elderly man" who had not developed a sophisticated understanding of the various ways print can be constructed. Similarly, Riojas Clark (1995) demonstrated via case studies that LEA was useful in teaching her bilingual students. Purcell-Gates and Waterman's (2000) adult students in El Salvador were also taught using the language experience approach in a Freirean-based class.

STEP-BY-STEP

Language experience approach has been successfully used with primary grade students and adults with little or no formal language. LEA can also be adapted for secondary school classrooms across the content areas. The purpose of LEA in secondary school classrooms is to allow learners to see their ideas and questions transformed into print. This written language serves as a record of their thinking as they learn. An added benefit is the support that comes for English language learners and those who are less comfortable with their ability to write. Using LEA, students see how academic and technical vocabulary is used in written form. Therefore, students need to see the print as it is scribed. While there are common features of an LEA lesson, the sequence varies slightly for secondary students.

1. Use a language chart or the whiteboard, and choose markers in cool colors (blue, green, black) that can be seen from a distance. Be sure to write large and legibly so that the students in the back of the room can see.
2. LEA lends itself to use in classroom discussions, so have your materials at the ready to capture their ideas. Begin by titling the chart, as this will serve as a way of organizing thinking.
3. As students contribute key ideas to the discussion, pause to focus on how the information is put onto the chart. Ask students to repeat or refine ideas, preferably in

complete sentences. Minimize the amount of paraphrasing you do, as the goal is to capture their language.

4. After the chart has been completed, ask students to read over what has been written. You may choose to continue instruction, using their ideas as a launching point for further development of concepts.

5. After additional instruction on the topic, ask students to reread what was written earlier on the language chart. Look for ideas and statements that need to be revised to reflect new learning. Write these as well, and ask students to check for accuracy.

6. When possible, keep these charts on display during the unit of instruction. Date the charts so that students can follow the development of their understanding of the topic. Begin classes with a rereading of the charts, which will serve as an effective way to summarize content from the previous day's lesson.

APPLICATION AND EXAMPLES

Algebra teacher Meg Brandywine was concerned that her students could not correctly solve word problems. She knew that they needed to be able to read the problem, to understand the vocabulary, to identify the necessary equation, and so forth. She knew how to teach them those things. Her frustration centered on her students' inability to set up the problem—to identify the first thing they needed to do. Her solution was to slow down the "problem-solving" process. Using the language experience approach, Ms. Brandywine projected a word problem on the overhead. She invited her students to talk about the problem. From there, they would agree on the first step in solving the problem. When they did so, Ms. Brandywine served as their collective scribe and recorded their response on the whiteboard.

In a physics class, Ms. Greene wanted to encourage her students to write more accurate statements in their notes. Ms. Greene used LEA to focus her students on the difference between main ideas, important details, and supporting information. During a lecture on Newton's first law, Ms. Greene paused and discussed the content with her students. Together, they identified specific things that should appear in their notes. They knew that Newton's first law is stated as "An object at rest stays at rest" and "an object in motion tends to stay in motion, unless acted on by an unbalanced force." During their discussion, they decided on a note, which read (and Ms. Greene wrote), "Objects keep on doing what they're doing." In discussing the idea of unbalanced forces, they chose to focus on the example of their recent visit to the roller coasters and how they moved and stopped moving.

References

Ashton-Warner, S. (1963). *Teacher*. New York: Simon & Schuster.

Brehaut, L. (1994). Starting from scratch: Teaching an elderly man to read. *Good Practice in Australian Adult Literacy and Basic Education, 25*, 11–13, 15.

Fisher, D., & Frey, N. (2003). Writing instruction for struggling adolescent readers: A gradual release model. *Journal of Adolescent & Adult Literacy, 46*, 396–407.

Purcell-Gates, V., & Waterman, R. (2000). *Now we read, we see, we speak: Portrait of literacy development in an adult Freirean-based class*. Mahwah, NJ: Erlbaum.

Riojas Clark, E. (1995). "How did you learn to write in English when you haven't been taught in English?" The language experience approach in a dual language program. *Bilingual Research Journal, 19*, 611–627.

18

Mnemonics

A mnemonic device is a tool that helps a person transform or organize information to enhance its retrievability from memory (Belleza, 1983). Mnemonics can be used to learn and remember individual items (a name, a fact, a date), sets of information (a list of numbers, a list of vocabulary definitions, a shopping list, a sequence of events, names of the Great Lakes), procedures (order of operations in math, rules for capitalization), and ideas expressed in text.

These devices range from simple, easy-to-learn techniques to somewhat complex systems that require significant practice. Because they incorporate visual and verbal forms of encoding, the effectiveness of mnemonics is likely due to the systematic use of organization and meaningfulness. Although mnemonics are useful, sometimes it's much less work to simply write down the information that will need to be recalled.

The research evidence indicates that mnemonics are useful for students with and without disabilities (Elliott & Gentile, 1986), English language learners (Sener & Belfiore, 2005), people with memory loss (Cherry & Simmons-D'Gerolamo, 2005), and students who find school challenging (Goll, 2004). Students who create their own mnemonics outperform those who do not (Mastropieri & Scruggs, 1998). In sum, "remember TAMME (Teaching Acronyms Makes Memorizing Easy)" (Santaniello, 2005, p. 56). We also know that sometimes it's better to write things down. Figure 18.1 describes when it's best to use a mnemonics versus when it's best to write something down.

STEP-BY-STEP

1. For common mnemonics, use the Internet. There are a number of sites that provide lists of mnemonics such as *http://www.aidtomemory.com* or *http://en.wikipedia.org/wiki/Mnemonic.*
2. As you identify areas in your curriculum that cluster together, develop your own mnemonics. The key is to make the letter of the content match the letter of a common word and then put the words into a sentence that is easy to remember.
3. As students become familiar with the idea of mnemonics, invite them to create mnemonics on their own. Ask students to review several common mnemonics and to identify key features of these study tools as they create mnemonics of their own.

APPLICATION AND EXAMPLES

Some common mnemonics help students process information. For example, "Please Excuse My Dear Aunt Sally" provides students with specific information about solving math problems

Figure 18.1 When To Use a Mnemonic

When it's best to use a mnemonic

- when information needs to be remembered for only a short time
- as a reminder for well-learned information (to help overcome memory blocks; to remind you of the order of information)
- when written records are impossible, inconvenient, or inappropriate
- to anchor facts

When it's best to write something down

- when you need to remember the information for a long time
- when reliability and accuracy are important
- when memory load is to be avoided
- when information is coming at you too fast
- when the information is too complex

Source: From "Memory Guide," retrieved from *http://www.memory-key.com/mnemonics/mnemonics.htm.* Copyright © 2000–2005 Capital Research Limited. Used with permission.

with a specific order of operations: parentheses, exponents, multiplication, division, addition, and subtraction. And the acronym *SOH-CAH-TOA* (pronounced "soak a toe-uh") stands for:

SOH   **S**ine = **O**pposite leg divided by the **H**ypotenuse
CAH   **C**osine = **A**djacent leg divided by the **H**ypotenuse
TOA   **T**angent = **O**pposite leg divided by the **A**djacent leg

The students in Mr. Creswell's biology class like to find or create mnemonics for themselves. Mr. Creswell provides students with bonus points for writing their study mnemonics on the test. Here are some of the recent mnemonics his students used:

Biological Classifications: *Kings Play Chess On Fine Grain Sand* (Kingdom, Phylum, Class, Order, Family, Genus, Species).
Mitosis: *People Meet And Talk or "PMAT"* (Prophase, Metaphase, Anaphase, Telophase).
White Blood Cells: *Nobody Likes My Educational Background* (In order of decreasing numbers: Neutrophils, Lymphocytes, Monocytes, Eosinophils, and Basophils).
Six Forms of Energy: *SCREAM* (Sound, Chemical, Radiant [which includes Heat and Light], Electric, Atomic, and Mechanical).

References

Belleza, F. S. (1983). Mnemonic-device instruction with adults. In M. Pressley & J. R. Levin (Eds.), *Cognitive strategy research: Psychological foundations.* New York: Springer-Verlag.

Cherry, K., & Simmons-D'Gerolamo, S. S. (2005). Long-term effectiveness of spaced-retrieval memory training for older adults with probable Alzheimer's disease. *Experimental Aging Research, 31,* 261–289.

Elliott, J. L., & Gentile, J. R. (1986). The efficacy of a mnemonic technique for learning disabled and nondisabled adolescents. *Journal of Learning Disabilities, 19,* 237–241.

Goll, P. S. (2004). Mnemonic strategies: Creating schemata for learning enhancement. *Education, 125,* 306–312.

Mastropieri, M. A., & Scruggs, T. E. (1998). Enhancing school success with mnemonic strategies. *Intervention in School and Clinic, 33,* 201–208.

Santaniello, S. W. (2005). Don't forget acronyms. *Teaching PreK-8, 35*(8), 56–57.

Sener, U., & Belfiore, P. J. (2005). Mnemonics strategy development: Improving alphabetic understanding in Turkish students, at risk for failure in EFL settings. *Journal of Behavioral Education, 14,* 105–115.

19

Literacy Focus

Before Reading
During Reading
After Reading

Fluency
Comprehension
Vocabulary
Writing
Oral Language

Modeled Writing

A good way for students to reflect upon or extend new information is to use it to create a new text. However, some students find it difficult to write about what they know in traditional types of writing assignments, either because these assignments are not particularly motivating, or students are uncertain about how to get their thoughts on paper. The difficulties associated with academic writing often mask what students actually know and prevent students from realizing that writing is a way of thinking more about a topic. As Kirby, Kirby, and Liner (2004) put it, "Somehow students get the notion that the form of what they have to say takes precedence over *what* [italics added] they say—that is, over content" (p. 196).

Books and other texts with unique and distinctive formats often provide good models and scaffolds for student writing (Fisher & Frey, 2003). The idea behind modeled writing is to take new information gained from one context (e.g., reading, listening to a lecture, watching a movie, conducting an experiment) and transform it into a brand-new text, using an already published or existing text as a model for style and format.

STEP-BY-STEP

For modeled writing to be useful, students need access to a wide variety of books. From there, they need permission to use the structures they find in the books in their own writing. Beginning with a class discussion on the difference between plagiarism and modeled writing is helpful. Once these two steps have been completed, the use of modeled writing can be directly taught and encouraged.

1. Select a favorite text and read it aloud to students.
2. Show students the specific structures that the author used to create the text. This can be common text structures such as cause and effect or problem/solution or styles such as naming three items separated by commas.
3. Ask students to use the model and write their own pieces. Provide time for students to share their writing and reinforce that there is a wide range of writing possible from any given model.
4. Using sentence frames that you've created, encourage students to complete the writing. A sample frame, with a focus on the genre of fantasy, may read:

   I was walking home when _____. I couldn't believe it! I was actually seeing _____. There they/it were/was. As I turned the corner, I _____. And then, _____. But that's not the end. Later, _____.

APPLICATION AND EXAMPLES

After reading *Next Stop Neptune: Experiencing the Solar System* (Jenkins, 2004), Natasha decided to write what she learned about the planet Mars. Rather than having her write a traditional descriptive paragraph in which she would get caught up in the mechanics of writing, Natasha's science teacher helped her keep content at the forefront by providing a range of models for her writing. This student decided that Henry Cole's *I Took a Walk* (1998) would help her write about Mars, even though it dealt with a topic that differed from *Next Stop Neptune*. In this simple-to-read, but content-rich picture book, the narrator details his journey through the woods, into a meadow, and by a stream, stopping at each point to list his observations:

> I sat quietly at the edge of the pond and peered through the tall cattails. I saw . . . a grebe on her nest, a heron, whirligig beetles, a bluegill, tree swallows, a rail, a painted turtle, a damselfly, a marsh wren's nest, yellow iris, a dragonfly, a minnow, water lilies. (pp. 19–20)

Because much of what she read about Mars was descriptive in nature, Natasha felt this pattern was a good fit for her writing that would make it easy to share what she knew. She wrote the following short piece:

I took a walk on Mars

One spring morning, I took a walk on Mars.

I sat on a rock, and I saw . . .

Red, dusty soil

Craters

A big chasm called Valles Marineris

The Mars Rover

And the largest volcano on any planet

For Natasha, an inexperienced writer, this was the perfect scaffold. Modeled writing is particularly useful for crafting short pieces that highlight content, but it can also be used for writing longer texts (e.g., journal entry, memoir, newspaper article). The key to making models useful is to find texts that lend themselves to the content under consideration. Also, picture books in particular are good models because they often contain simple structures that inexperienced readers and writers would find both accessible and nonintimidating. Table 19.1 provides some additional examples of texts that can be used as models and that suit a range of topics.

Table 19.1 Modeled Writing Book List

Book	Format/Uses
Gordon, S. (2004). *Guess what changes?* New York: Benchmark Books.	• Descriptive hints on each page that lead to "Who am I?" (Answer: A butterfly) • Good model for describing a person (e.g., Andy Warhol), an event (e.g., Boxer Rebellion), a place (e.g., Japan), a concept (e.g., Pythagorean theorem), or a phenomenon (e.g., volcanic eruption).
Dunphy, M. (1999). *Here is the African Savannah.* New York: Hyperion.	• Cumulative text describing the relationships among plants and animals of the African Savannah. • Good model for writing about cycles (e.g., food chain) or sequences of events (e.g., connected events leading up to American Revolution).

Continued

Table 19.1 *continued*

Book	Format/Uses
Leedy, L. (1993). *Postcards from Pluto: A tour of the solar system*. New York: Holiday House.	• Series of postcards sent home from a group of kids on a trip to the solar system; includes details of what they learned. • Student-authored texts might include, for example, *Postcards from the Oregon Trail, Postcards from a WWII Concentration Camp, Postcards from the Mojave Desert*, and so on.
Wright-Frierson, V. (1998). *An island scrapbook: Dawn to dusk on a barrier island*. New York: Aladdin.	• Mix of narrative text, labeled sketches, lists, and observations. • Student-authored texts might include, for example, *A Japanese Internment Camp Scrapbook, A Metropolitan Museum Scrapbook, An Ellis Island Scrapbook*, and so forth.
Janeczko, P. B. (2001). *A poke in the I: A collection of concrete poems*. Cambridge, MA: Candlewick Press.	• Each poem is written in the shape of the poem's topic (e.g., poem about an Eskimo Pie written in that shape). • Good model for writing about the concrete and visual (e.g., octagon, saxophone, kidney).
Stamaty, M. A. (2004). *Alia's mission: Saving the books of Iraq*. New York: Knopf.	• True story told in comic strip/graphic format. • Good model for students with artistic strengths. Drawings serve as scaffolds for writing.
Avery, P. (2003). *Letters from Korea: A story of the Korean War*. Kimberling City, MO: River Road Press.	• Fictional letters based on real people, events, and photographs. • Good model for writing firsthand accounts of events (e.g., Battle of Bull Run), phenomena (flood), or specific conditions (e.g., quality of Depression-era life).

References

Cole, H. (1998). *I took a walk*. New York: Greenwillow Books.

Fisher, D., & Frey, N. (2003). Writing instruction for struggling adolescent readers: A gradual release model. *Journal of Adolescent & Adult Literacy, 46*, 396–407.

Jenkins, A. (2004). *Next stop Neptune: Experiencing the solar system*. Boston: Houghton Mifflin.

Kirby, D., Kirby, D. L., & Liner, T. (2004). *Inside out: Strategies for teaching writing* (3rd ed.). Portsmouth, NH: Heinemann.

20

Literacy Focus

⬭ Before Reading	⬛ Fluency
⬛ During Reading	⬛ Comprehension
⬭ After Reading	⬭ Vocabulary
	⬭ Writing
	⬭ Oral Language

Modeling Language of Process

One of the most challenging aspects of teaching is making obvious to students what comes natural to us. With most everything we read, whether for work or pleasure, meaning is automatic. Because it's so automatic it's difficult even to know how we process text and, therefore, how to describe the process to others. And yet, allowing youth to eavesdrop on our thinking while we make meaning from the disciplinary texts we require them to read is a critical part of our work (Bransford, Brown, & Cocking, 2000; Kintsch & Kintsch, 2005). What we're describing is not unlike the master–apprentice relationship in the trades. A master electrician, for example, demonstrates a wiring technique for an assistant while explaining *why* it's done, *how* it's done, and *what* is needed to complete the job. Imagine, then, reading with students and explaining to them *why* you're reading a certain way, *how* you're making meaning of the text, and *what* students will need to do to be equally successful when they read (Greenleaf, Schoenbach, Cziko, & Mueller, 2001). Teachers and students can do this if they have a common language—that is, a language of process.

STEP-BY-STEP

Teaching students a way of labeling the thought processes that go into making meaning from text requires developing a habit of talking about how the material is being read as much as what is being read (Caccamise & Snyder, 2005). Talking about how the material is being read is what we call the *language of process*.

1. Become aware of the typical cognitive and metacognitive processes expert readers use. There are many well-researched cognitive and metacognitive activities all good readers engage in to ensure effective meaning making (see Figure 20.1).
2. Practice documenting and/or verbalizing the use of these mental processes while reading.
3. Share with students the list of common mental processes expert readers use when constructing meaning from text.
4. With a common text, read aloud paragraphs and sections, pausing periodically to talk about what it is you're understanding about the text (referred to as *content statements*) and how you're reaching those understandings based on the common mental processes (referred to as *process statements*).
5. Making content and process statements will have to occur regularly and frequently in order to provide youth with appropriate repetition.

Figure 20.1 Common Mental Processes Expert Readers Use

- Making and checking predictions
- Forming mental images
- Connecting to experience
- Summarizing and paraphrasing
- Analyzing text structure
- Verbalizing points of confusion and employing fix-up strategies
- Using contextual clues for word learning

6. Have students pair up and, using a shared text, trade off reading paragraphs and verbalize both content and process statements with one another.
7. The goal is for these mental operations to become so routinized and automatic for students while they read that the need to verbalize them will no longer be necessary.

APPLICATION AND EXAMPLES

Figure 20.2 displays content and process statements teachers have made about texts from a variety of disciplines. These statements can serve as a model for other teachers as they learn to develop a language of process for communicating about what is read and how it is read to their students.

Figure 20.2 Various Disciplinary Teachers' Content and Process Statements

Making and Checking Predictions

Content Statement for a Chapter on Weather in Science

In this next part, I think we'll find out why the men flew into the hurricane.

Process Statement

*This is my way of **predicting** what might happen next. And now as I continue to read, I'll pay close attention to see if my prediction is correct or not.*

Forming Mental Images

Content Statement for Shakespeare's *Hamlet* in English

Okay, Hamlet's ship has been pirated and he's left on the shore without his possessions.

Process Statement

What I'm doing here is forming a picture in my mind of this scene, a mental image, so I can see what's happening and better understand it.

Connecting to Experience

Content Statement for Jack London's *To Build a Fire*

So he's lost in the woods with nothing to make a fire . . .

Process Statement

I can understand what he's going through because I went through a similar experience when I was a teenager. . . . By relating the story to my own experience I can see how the events fit together and make more sense out of them.

Summarizing and Paraphrasing

Content Statement for a Chapter on Presidential Politics in History

In this section it says Jesse Jackson reached out to farmers, factory workers, and mainstream democrats in his bid for the 1988 presidential nomination.

Continued

Figure 20.2 *continued*

Process Statement

So, what does this mean? Apparently, Jackson broadened his political base in the 1988 election and made a much more serious bid for the presidency. What I tried to do was to summarize this section by putting it in my own words, or to paraphrase it.

Analyzing Text Structure

Content Statement for a Pamphlet on CPR in Health

So maybe it wasn't such a good idea to try the Heimlich maneuver in that situation.

Process Statement

I'm looking at the expression "on the other hand" and it tells me the author wants me to consider another side to this issue. By analyzing the structure of the text, I can get a better idea of the author's intent.

Verbalizing Points of Confusion and Employing Fix-Up Strategies

Content Statement for an Essay on Human Evolution by Stephen J. Gould

Gould says the earliest known hominid was 4 million years old, but just a couple of paragraphs before he said homo sapiens *were 2 million years old.*

Process Statement

I'm confused. . . . I'd better reread to check this again. But if that doesn't help, maybe if I read ahead it will become clearer.

Using Contextual Clues for Word Learning

Content Statement for a Newspaper Article in Journalism

Right here in the article it states that the propinquity of the paint store caused the fire to spread rapidly.

Process Statement

The word propinquity *is new to me; what about you? I'm going to read the sentence before and after this one again to see if the context provides clues to its meaning.*

References

Bransford, J., Brown, A., & Cocking, R. (2000). *How people learn: Brain, mind, experience, and school* (expanded edition). Washington, DC: National Academy Press.

Caccamise, D., & Snyder, L. (2005). Theory and pedagogical practices of text comprehension. *Topics in Language Disorders, 25,* 5–20.

Greenleaf, C., Schoenbach, R., Cziko, C., & Mueller, F. (2001). Apprenticing adolescent readers to academic literacy. *Harvard Educational Review, 71,* 79–127.

Kintsch, W., & Kintsch, E. (2005). Comprehension. In S. Paris & S. Stahl (Eds.), *Current issues on reading comprehension and assessment* (pp. 71–92). Mahwah, NJ: Erlbaum.

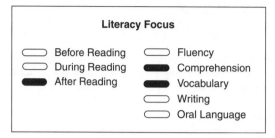

Literacy Focus

◯ Before Reading	◯ Fluency
◯ During Reading	⬛ Comprehension
⬛ After Reading	⬛ Vocabulary
	◯ Writing
	◯ Oral Language

Opinionnaire

An opinionnaire is a tool for eliciting attitudes about a topic (Smagorinsky, McCann, & Kern, 1987). These are most commonly used as a prereading activity, and are designed to "help students to broaden their repertoire of interpretive strategies by encouraging them to consider and evaluate authors' and characters' uses of important themes and ideas and by helping them to connect literature and life" (White & Johnson, 2001, p. 120).

Opinionnaires have been widely used as a tool for measurement in the social sciences and in medicine since the 1930s (Shaw & Wright, 1967). Classroom application of opinionnaires has been altered to focus on seeking opinions, rather than as the measurement tool used by social scientists. This prereading activity has been used in an American history course to debate the impact of Columbus on the Western Hemisphere (O'Connor & Como, 1998) and to promote discussion on Bradbury's (1967) short story "The Veldt" in a high school literature class (Johannessen, 1992).

Formats for opinionnaires vary, but all feature a series of statements that are meant to be provocative or controversial. For example, Johannessen's opinionnaire developed for "The Veldt" has statements such as "Technological advances make life better for everyone" (1992, p. 50). Johnson asked her students, who were reading *The Giver* (Lowry, 1993), to comment on statements such as "Our society is too complicated; one based on simple right and wrong would be better" (White & Johnson, 2001, p. 122).

Most opinionnaires do not allow for a neutral response, either asking for an agree/disagree response, or one that provides further degrees of opinion, such as strongly agree/agree/disagree/strongly disagree. Some teachers also provide space for students to provide a reason for their opinion. An example of this format appears in Figure 21.1.

Opinionnaires can be used in several ways. For instance, they may be used as both a pre- and postreading activity, where students can express a change of opinion based on new information. They may be used to elicit information from the class about a particular topic, such as an earth science teacher distributing opinionnaires to measure the level of concern about several environmental issues. Literature teachers can use opinionnaires that ask for the thoughts of several characters in a novel. For example, how might the character Odysseus of *The Odyssey* respond to the statement, "The end justifies the means"? What might his wife Penelope say?

STEP-BY-STEP

1. Create an opinionnaire of no more than 10 statements. This allows students time to think carefully about their opinions, rather than rushing through a long list. The statements should be strongly stated, and worthy of debate. Adolescents crave this kind of mental challenge, so use their opinions to generate interest in your content.

Figure 21.1 Opinionnaire

Name _____   Period _____

Directions: Read each statement below and indicate whether you agree (A) or disagree (D). Write your reason for your opinion as well. There are no "right answers."

_____ A society is safest when its laws are strictly enforced.
Your reason:

_____ All citizens have a right to bear arms so they can protect themselves.
Your reason:

_____ In times of war, the military should be able to use private property.
Your reason:

_____ Free speech needs to be protected, even if it is against the government.
Your reason:

_____ There are times when a criminal should be put to death.
Your reason:

_____ There are times when the police should be allowed to seize evidence against a criminal.
Your reason:

---

2. Determine whether you want to offer a dichotomous choice (agree/disagree) or a Likert scale(strongly agree/agree/disagree/strongly disagree). The Likert scale is best for opinionnaires that ask for opinions that are more complex.
3. Consider whether you want students to explain themselves. Insight into their reasoning can be helpful for you as you shape your lessons. However, asking for reasons on more sensitive issues may be viewed as intrusive.
4. You may want to make the opinionnaires anonymous, so that you can elicit more truthful answers. Many students will tell you what they think you want to hear at the expense of their own ideas. Remind them that there are no right or wrong answers.
5. Opinionnaires lead quite naturally into discussion, so allow time for this to develop. Review the rules for debate in your class, especially as they relate to the opinions of others.
6. Choose a reading to follow the opinionnaire. This tool is meant to stimulate their interpretive reasoning and background knowledge, but even well-tilled soil needs a seed. The reading should be interesting and provoke thought about the statements in the opinionnaire, as well as provide new information for consideration.
7. Follow the reading with further discussion about the topic. Encourage students to use evidence from the text to support their arguments. Unlike the first discussion, personal opinion alone should not carry the day.
8. Give students the opportunity to revisit their opinions. If you asked for reasons the first time, then do so the second time as well.

APPLICATION AND EXAMPLES

Mr. Djenonyombaye will be teaching his eighth-grade social studies students about the U.S. Constitution and the Bill of Rights, but he first wants them to understand the moral and ethical struggles of the founders as they crafted a constitution for the new country. He begins by explaining that the constitutional convention lasted 4 months and was marked by much debate and disagreement among the 55 delegates. Even then, not all the delegates agreed, and some refused to send it to their states for ratification until a list of the rights of all citizens was included.

Mr. Djenonyombaye then tells his students that he wants them to wrestle with some of the ideas Congress had to debate in designing this list of rights. "You all have opinions, just like those people did in 1789, I'd like you to read these statements and think about your opinions. Decide whether you agree or disagree, and write your reason. No answer is right or wrong—this is your opinion," he explains. The opinionnaire he used is shown in Figure 21.1.

The class then discussed the items on the opinionnaire and offered a wide range of ideas. Gabriel commented, "If our country is under attack, the army needs to be able to go wherever it needs to."

"My dad's in Iraq, and he says that it can be dangerous to let a military do that. What if they just showed up at your house and kicked out your whole family?" challenges Jenny.

Mr. Djenonyombaye is pleased with the liveliness of the debate and knows that his Bill of Rights unit is off to a great start. Soon, the students will be reading primary source documents and informational texts regarding the Bill of Rights. Their first reading will be from their textbook, as they review the Bill of Rights and basic information about its development. At the end of this 2-week unit, they will revisit their opinionnaires and debate the issues once again.

References

Bradbury, R. (1967). *The illustrated man* ("The Veldt," pp. 7–18). New York: Bantam Books.

Johannessen, L. R. (1992). Using an opinionnaire to promote discussion in a literature class. *The Clearing House, 66*(1), 47–50.

Lowry, L. (1993). *The giver*. New York: Laurel Leaf.

O'Connor, J. S., & Como, R. M. (1998). History on trial: The case of Columbus. *Organization of American Historians Magazine of History, 12*(2), 45–48.

Shaw, M. E., & Wright, J. M. (1967). *Scales for the measurement of attitudes*. New York: McGraw-Hill.

Smagorinsky, P., McCann, T., & Kern, S. (1987). *Explorations: Introductory activities for literature and composition*. Urbana, IL: National Council of Teachers of English.

White, B., & Johnson, T. S. (2001). We really do mean it: Implementing language arts standard #3 with opinionnaires. *The Clearing House, 74*(3), 119–123.

Literacy Focus

⬤ Before Reading	◯ Fluency
◯ During Reading	⬤ Comprehension
◯ After Reading	⬤ Vocabulary
	◯ Writing
	◯ Oral Language

Pattern Guide

Pattern guides are visual representations of the text structure used in a passage. These are most commonly used with informational pieces that exhibit clear structures, such as cause and effect, compare/contrast, temporal sequence, problem/solution, or description (see Strategy 42, "Text Structures," for more information). Pattern guides were originally described by Herber (1970), and have since enjoyed a useful reputation in middle and high school classrooms (Wood, Lapp, & Flood, 1992). Teachers like them because they encourage students to focus on the relationships between concepts, and students appreciate the hands-on nature of this strategy. The pattern guide in Figure 22.1 is an example of one used in a middle school science class.

The intent of a pattern guide is not to merely match facts or concepts with one another. After all, a simple understanding of jigsaw puzzles is all one would need to accomplish this. Rather, pattern guides should be used in conjunction with a piece of text. One application is as an advance organizer for preparing for the reading. Students can be given the individual pieces of the pattern guide as part of a discussion on the concepts to be read, then used to assemble during the reading. As well, students can create their own pattern guides as a form of review. Another review technique is to distribute individual pieces of the patterns to each student in the class. They must locate the matching pieces and discuss the relationships between the facts or concepts. The pieces of a pattern guide can be distributed to students. Ultimately, students should use a pattern guide to incorporate the information into an expository piece of their own creation.

STEP-BY-STEP

1. Choose a passage from a textbook or other assigned reading that lends itself to a pattern guide. Look for signal words to identify these relationships. Keep in mind that most texts use a variety of structures to explain concepts and relationships to one another, so choose examples that are fairly straightforward.
2. Develop a pattern guide of interlocking pieces. We have found that blackline masters for graphic organizers can be a good source for patterns. Cut the pattern pieces apart and organize them in envelopes or small self-sealing plastic bags.
3. Distribute the pattern guides to the students and provide an overview of the concepts that will be featured in the reading. Remind students to look for signal words associated with text structures (see Strategy 42). Tell students that as they read, they should assemble the pattern guide. Point out that if they have not located a piece of information represented on the guide, they should reread the passage.
4. Tell students what you would like them to do with the pattern guides after the reading. Possible follow-up activities include:
   - Glue pieces to their notebook and add information gleaned from the reading, classroom activities, and demonstrations.

Figure 22.1 Description Pattern Guide for Middle School Science

Match the descriptions to the correct body system.

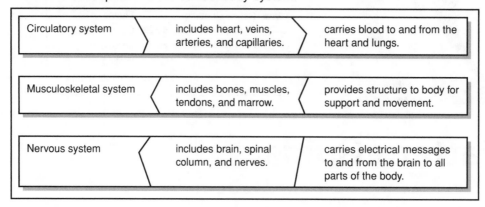

- Redistribute pieces so that each student has one piece of the pattern guide. Instruct them to locate other students who have interlocking pieces. These small groups should discuss or write about the information represented in their pattern.
- Invite students to use the pattern guide as a device for recalling information in an oral explanation of the concepts.
- Use the pattern guide as an organizer for a paragraph of explanation or an essay related to the topic.

APPLICATION AND EXAMPLES

Mr. Anzelone's 10th-grade world history students have been reading about the events in Europe leading up to World War II. Today's passage covering the rapidly unfolding drama of 1939–1940 has been confusing to students in previous years, so he has decided to use a strategy new to the class to help them with the material. He has developed a pattern guide and notetaking page to insert into their World History binders (see Figure 22.2). After distributing the pattern guide, he reviews its purpose.

"Events on the European continent just before World War II caused significant change in the balance of power. You'll be reading about and discussing these events in class today and tomorrow. I've put together a tool to assist you in learning this critical information," he explains.

Mr. Anzelone tells them that the predominant structure used in this portion of the text is temporal (time or chronology-base) sequence and reminds them to notice signal words such as *first, next,* and *finally* as they read. "You've always heard me say that understanding history is much more than lining up events and dates. However, it is essential that you witness how rapidly these events took place in order to understand the shock of the world community. That shock led to paralysis by many world leaders, including Britain, the United States, and France. I want us to know these events first, so we can more fully discuss why these leaders responded as they did," he says.

After taking a few minutes for students to cut apart the pattern guide, Mr. Anzelone explains that they will reassemble these pieces as they read. He reviews each item and gives them some insights into the significance of each, then asks them to read three pages of the text. "Put the pattern guide together as you read," he tells them. "This will help you keep track of the information."

After the students complete the reading, Mr. Anzelone leads a discussion of the events. He is interested in reviewing the sequence of events before class ends, so he distributes a second set of pattern guide pieces he prepared in advance. "Take your pattern piece and find six other people to complete your sequence. I want all of you to discuss these events because you'll have a homework assignment on this tonight."

After several minutes of lively discussion, Mr. Anzelone asks the students to return to their seats. "The last thing I want you to do with this is to add notes and important ideas in the lines spaces next to each event. Put all of this in your History binder because we'll use this again later in your writing."

Figure 22.2 Pattern Guide for High School World History

Directions: Events in Europe in 1939 and 1940 were pivotal in the eventual involvement of the United States in WWII. Read the passage in your textbook on pages 135–137 and assemble this information in your social studies notebook. Look for signal words that show the chronological order of the events.

1. _____	1. Hitler annexes Austria and claims that 99% of Austrians support this change (p. 135).
2. _____	2. French and British sign the Munich Pact with Germany, allowing for the annexation of part of Czechoslovakia. Chamberlain announces that this will allow for "peace for our time" (p. 136).
3. _____	3. Kristallnacht, a program of terror targeting German Jews, results in the 25,000 sent to concentration camps (p. 136).
4. _____	4. Germany invades the rest of Czechoslovakia, and Italy attacks Albania (p. 137).
5. _____	5. Germany invades Poland (p. 137).
6. _____	6. Charles Lindbergh urges Americans to support a policy of isolation to prevent involvement with European turmoil (p. 137).
7. _____	7. Poland is divided among Germany and Soviet Russia (p. 137).

At the end of the week, Mr. Anzelone asks them to use the information from the pattern guide in a new way. In the days after this lesson, they have learned more about the responses of the American, British, and French governments to these events. "I'd like you to take the position of one of these governments and defend the decisions made. Use your pattern guide to refer to specfic events, and be sure to explain why these decisions were made in light of the timeline," he tells them. Later, Mr. Anzelone remarked, "I was really happy with the way this came together. When I first heard about pattern guides, I thought it was too simple for 11th graders. But I've seen how they have used them. I don't want them to think history is just being able to reel off dates and names. But I also know that they need to analyze history through a chronological lens. The pattern guide has let me build this basis of information so they can get to the higher levels of analysis and evaluation."

References

Herber, H. L. (1970). *Teaching reading in the content areas*. Upper Saddle River, NJ: Prentice Hall.
Wood, K. D., Lapp, D., & Flood, J. (1992). *Guiding readers through text: A review of study guides*. Newark, DE: International Reading Association.

23

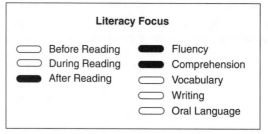

Poems for Two Voices

Longtime favorites in English class poetry studies have been Fleischman's Newberry Medal winner *Joyful Noise: Poems for Two Voices* (1988), which deals with the insect world, and his earlier volume *I Am Phoenix: Poems for Two Voices* (1985), which is a celebration of birds. Pappas uses the two-voice format to introduce mathematical terms and concepts in *Math Talk: Mathematical Ideas in Poems for Two Voices* (1991). Students love the sound of these cleverly crafted poems that are designed to be read aloud by two voices, sometimes alternating and sometimes simultaneously.

However, poems for two voices have some added benefits that can be used to help students consider text structures and an alternative form of writing. They are often set up to tell two sides of a story or to compare and contrast two concepts or experiences. For instance, consider the beginning of "Honeybees" from *Joyful Noise:*

Being a bee	Being a bee
	Is a joy
Is a pain	
	I'm a queen
I'm a worker	
I'll gladly explain.	I'll gladly explain. (p. 29)

The remainder of the poem details the disparate lives of the worker bee and queen bee. This kind of text serves as a perfect model for comparing and contrasting content-related ideas in classes other than English.

STEP-BY-STEP

1. Share poems for two voices as you would echo or choral reading (see Strategy 7).
2. Ask students to divide into two groups to read the poem in columns as they are written.
3. When students are familiar with this format of poem, they can be encouraged to use this style of writing to compare and contrast things they are reading.

APPLICATION AND EXAMPLES

In a science class, this format can be used to compare two different biomes using a text series such as Johnson's *A Walk in the Deciduous Forest* (2001a) and *A Walk in the Tundra* (2001b). Students might use a chart like the one in Table 23.1 to record information as they read that includes the following categories: climate, ground cover, plants, animals, what I might see, and what I might hear.

Table 23.1 Data Collection Chart

Category of Information	Tundra	Deciduous Forest
Climate	Cold, dry, harsh climate; a long, cold, dark winter, and a short summer.	Moist, mild climate; four distinct seasons.
Ground cover	Frozen most of the year; even in the summer, portions of the ground never thaw (permafrost). Constant thawing and melting makes ground cracked and lumpy.	Rich, dark soil covered in snow in the winter; wildflowers in the spring; moss, lacy ferns, and poison ivy in the summer; and glowing red, yellow, and orange leaves in the autumn.
Plants	Low growing and crowded together; white anemone, poppies, campion flowers, lichens.	Oak trees, hickories, paper birches, walnut trees; Virginia creeper, wild grape, and bittersweet vines; mushrooms.
Animals	Lemmings (mouselike) are everywhere; arctic hares, arctic foxes, ptarmigans, polar bears, musk oxen.	Centipedes, pill bugs, snails, warblers, woodpeckers, gray squirrels, great horned owls, green snakes, black snakes, frogs, salamanders, gray foxes.
What I might see	A snowy owl preying on an arctic fox.	Chipmunks leaping from branch to branch; a rabbit hiding from a mink or weasel.
What I might hear	Lemmings rustling in the grass; a musk oxen snorting and stomping at an enemy.	The snorting call of a white-tailed deer.

It is important for students to focus first on learning the information through reading. Once students have compared the two biomes, they can then use their notes from the chart to make decisions about how to highlight important information in a two-part poem.

In history class, after reading about Martin Luther King and Malcolm X in *Now Is Your Time: The African-American Struggle for Freedom* (Myers, 1991), Dwayne created a Venn diagram to analyze the similarities and differences between these two important civil rights activists. He then used his graphic organizer to create a poem for two voices, one voice highlighting the life of King, and the other focusing on the life of Malcolm X. The phrases he used to describe the unique traits and experiences of each man were used to create the solo lines, and the commonalities between the men were used to write the sections to be read in unison. Like Fleischman, Dwayne even chose to have his voices represent different ideas spoken at the same time:

Martin Luther King	Malcolm X
	Born Malcolm Little
In the South	In the North
Civil Rights Movement	Civil Rights Movement
Christian	
	Muslim
Had a dream	Had a dream
Racial harmony	
	Racial separation
Nonviolent	
	By any means possible
Assassinated	Assassinated

Dwayne's teacher might have decided to have him write a compare-and-contrast essay on these two men, but the writing would not have been nearly as engaging, and it would not have been geared to any audience other than the teacher. On the other hand, Dwayne wrote this piece enthusiastically and then enlisted a classmate to help him read for his peers, all of whom enjoyed the performance and truly understood the gist of his writing.

In English class, a poem for two voices might be used to analyze inner conflict in literature. A twist on the poem for two voices is to combine it with the found poem concept. For instance, consider this *found poem for two voices* highlighting the inner turmoil of the main character in *Catalyst* (Anderson, 2002):

On the outside

                    On the inside

I am Good Kate

                    I am Bad Kate

Rev. Jack Malone's girl

                    Daughter of no one

Helps with the house

                    Prays with eyes open

Smart

                    Disrespectful

Honor roll

                    Disagreeable

So good with her brother

                    She's going to lose it. (pp. 3–4)

References

Anderson, L. H. (2002). *Catalyst*. New York: Viking Press.

Fleischman, P. (1985). *I am phoenix: Poems for two voices*. New York: HarperCollins.

Fleischman, P. (1988). *Joyful noise: Poems for two voices*. New York: HarperCollins.

Johnson, R. L. (2001a). *A walk in the deciduous forest*. Minneapolis, MN: Carolrhoda Books.

Johnson, R. L. (2001b). *A walk in the tundra*. Minneapolis, MN: Carolrhoda Books.

Myers, W. D. (1991). *Now is your time! The African-American struggle for freedom*. New York: Harper Trophy.

Pappas, T. (1991). *Math talk: Mathematical ideas in poems for two voices*. San Carlos, CA: World Wide Tetra.

24

Popcorn Review

Another strategy that creates a novel context for generative, student-directed rehearsal of newly learned content is popcorn review. The strategy gets its name from students "popping up" during the review process to state a fact or detail. This is followed by other students popping up in a random fashion to add related information, another fact in a sequence, or a subsequent story event.

While the teacher sets the popcorn review process in motion, students assume responsibility for prompting each other and holding each other accountable for what they've learned (Topping & Ehly, 1998). In this way, the strategy is designed to capitalize on the benefits of students teaching their peers (Mayer, 2002; Rubin & Hebert, 1995) through a fun and participatory activity.

STEP-BY-STEP

Popcorn review is a strategy that follows shortly after students have learned new content. The following description of steps assumes students are rehearsing their recall of material just covered:

1. Arrange the desks so there is a cluster of four or five grouped together at the front of the room.
2. Invite four or five students to take a seat in the desks at the front of the room.
3. Ask a student to stand and state a fact or event. For example, if the topic of the rock cycle has just been studied, a student might say "Magma forms through compaction and sedimentation."
4. Ask another student to pop up and state a fact that elaborates on the previous one or another step in a sequence or event in a story. For example, if a student stated "Hitler attacked Poland in May of 1939" the next student might say "The war in Poland lasted only 6 weeks." Yet another student might pop up and offer, "Hitler's army next marched into France," and so on.
5. Students participating in the popcorn review should be held accountable by their classmates, who should be checking for accuracy and interjecting with relevant information when appropriate.
6. Every few minutes, invite a new group of students to conduct the popcorn review. In this way everyone must be ready to participate in the process.
7. Redundancy of information stated by students should be acceptable; however, it may be necessary to propel the review in certain new directions on occasion. This can be done by supplying the first statement to get the popcorn review going.

APPLICATION AND EXAMPLES

Students in an English class hold popcorn review sessions frequently. Their teacher demonstrated the strategy early in the school year so that afterward she only needs to get her students started. In fact, her students enjoy the activity so much they often request it as their preferred way to review stories, novels, and other content.

After reading the Sherlock Holmes story "The Man with the Twisted Lip" (Doyle, 1930), she had her students assemble four chairs in two short rows in the middle of the classroom. Needing little encouragement, four volunteers eagerly took the seats. Shortly after getting settled, one of the students stood up and said, "The beggar Boone looked out the window of the opium house." Popping up immediately afterward another student added, "Just then his wife looked up and saw him."

This statement was followed by a third student's contribution: "Boone screamed and his wife started pounding on the door of the opium house." Then the fourth student offered: "When she couldn't get in she went for the police, who came to investigate."

At this point, the teacher stopped the four students and confirmed with the rest of the class that the statements were accurate retellings. She then thanked the students and asked for four more volunteers to replace them.

References

Doyle, A. C. (1930). *The complete Sherlock Holmes*. New York: Doubleday.

Mayer, R. E. (2002). Rote versus meaningful learning. *Theory Into Practice, 41,* 226–233.

Rubin, L., & Hebert, H. (1995). Model for active learning: Collaborative peer teaching. *College Teaching, 46,* 26–30.

Topping, K., & Ehly, S. (1998). *Peer-assisted learning.* Mahwah, NJ: Erlbaum.

25

Professor Know-It-All

There are many novel contexts for review and generative learning in the content classroom (Paris & Paris, 2001; Zimmerman, 2002). The best ones are those that position students as "experts" on topics to inform their peers and be challenged and held accountable by them (Boekaerts, Pintrich, & Zeidner, 2000; Spratt & Leung, 2000). One such strategy is called *professor know-it-all*. As the name suggests, students assume roles of know-it-alls or experts who are to provide answers to questions posed by their classmates. This approach has many benefits. First, students must be well versed in the content; second, students learn to ask a variety of questions at different levels of difficulty; and third, the strategy requires active participation on the part of all students.

STEP-BY-STEP

1. Once coverage of content has been completed, the professor know-it-all strategy can be enacted. The strategy is appropriate after reading a short story, a chapter from a novel or textbook, a lecture or presentation, a field trip, a film, or any other information source.
2. Form groups of three or four students. Give them time to review the content just covered. Tell them they will be called on randomly to come to the front of the room and provide expert answers to questions from their peers about the content.
3. Also ask the groups to generate three to five questions about the content they might anticipate being asked and that they can ask other experts.
4. To add a level of novelty to the strategy, some teachers keep on hand ties, graduation caps and gowns, lab coats, clipboards, or other symbols of professional expertise for students to don when it's their turn to be know-it-alls.
5. Call a group to the front of the room and ask them to face the class standing shoulder to shoulder.
6. Invite questions from the other groups. Students should ask their prepared questions first, then add others if more information is desired.
7. When the strategy is first employed, demonstrate with the class how you would like the professor know-it-alls to respond to their peers' questions. Typically, students are asked to huddle after receiving a question, discuss briefly how to answer it, then have the know-it-all spokesperson give the answer.
8. Remind students asking the questions to think carefully about the answers received and challenge or correct the professor know-it-alls if answers were not correct or need elaboration and amending.
9. After 5 minutes or so, ask a new group of professor know-it-alls to take their place in front of the class, and continue the process of students questioning students.

10. Initially, it may be necessary and helpful to model the various types of questions expected from students about the content. For example, students should ask the know-it-alls both factual and higher-level questions.

APPLICATION AND EXAMPLES

A health teacher employs the professor know-it-all strategy frequently to increase student engagement and increase the level of responsibility in their own learning. After the class read an article on the dangers of performance enhancement drugs, he asked students to form groups of four. Each student was expected to become expert on a particular aspect of the article. Groups were also instructed to think up four good questions about the content of the article to ask the know-it-alls. Because the health class had experience with the strategy, students got to work quickly while the teacher rotated throughout the room answering questions and providing any requested assistance.

The teacher then called on a group to put on lab coats and assume their positions in front of the classroom. Students from each of the other groups asked questions as did the teacher. The procedure for answering by the know-it-alls entailed gathering in a tight, closed circle to confer, decide on an answer, then recite the answer with each of the four students saying a word of a complete sentence. The teacher used this approach to reinforce the importance of thinking and speaking in complete thoughts.

For example, the know-it-alls were asked: "What are the side effects of taking steroids?" The response was: "The-side-effects-of-taking-steroids-include-different-kinds-of-cancer-sterility-and-psychological-disorders."

References

Boekaerts, M., Pintrich, P. R., & Zeidner, M. (2000). *Handbook of self-regulation* (pp. 13–39). San Diego, CA: Academic Press.

Paris, S. G., & Paris, A. H. (2001). Classroom applications of research on self-regulated learning. *Educational Psychologist, 36*, 89–101.

Spratt, M., & Leung, B. (2000). Peer teaching and peer learning revisited. *ELT Journal, 54*, 218–226.

Zimmerman, B. J. (2002). Becoming a self-regulated learner: An overview. *Theory Into Practice, 41*, 64–70.

26

Literacy Focus

⬭ Before Reading   ⬭ Fluency
⬭ During Reading   ⬛ Comprehension
⬛ After Reading   ⬭ Vocabulary
                     ⬭ Writing
                     ⬭ Oral Language

Questioning the Author

Questioning the Author (QtA) is a strategy that encourages readers to interact with information and build meaning from the text by analyzing the author's purpose in writing (Beck, McKeown, Hamilton, & Kucan, 1997). These questions, referred to as queries by Beck et al., are meant to serve as discussion prompts that allow students to develop their own ideas and not simply restate information directly from the text. QtA queries require that students take responsibility for their thinking and for constructing meaning (Beck & McKeown, 2001). Over time, students realize that the author is challenging them to build their own ideas and concepts as they interact with the ideas and concepts of the author (Beck & McKeown, 2002). Figure 26.1 contains a table of QtA queries.

The goals of QtA are always the same: to construct meaning of text, to help the student go beyond the words on the page, and to relate outside experiences from other texts. The means to the goal is discussion enriched by students and their own individual, personal histories. QtA involves the teachers as well as the class as they collaboratively build understanding during the reading. During QtA the teacher participates in the discussion as a facilitator, guide, initiator, and responder. The teacher does not dominate the conversation, but leads students into dialogue. The teacher strives to elicit the readers' thinking while keeping them focused in their discussion (McKeown & Beck, 1999). The students' answers are not evaluated in this procedure because QtA is designed to engage the readers with the text, not to rate the accuracy of their responses.

STEP-BY-STEP

As noted in Figure 26.1, there are specific goals associated with Questioning the Author (Beck, et al., 1997). These goals help identify the specific steps that should be followed so that students learn to ask questions of the author as they read.

1. The first step is to find reading material that will generate a good conversation. No strategy can compensate for boring and dry reading material.
2. Students need to be taught that they can, and should, ask questions of authors. Make a poster from the information in Figure 26.1 and teach students the types of questions that you expect them to ask. Over time, they'll add their own questions.
3. Discuss differences of opinion with students. Many of the authors that they will be asking questions of won't really give them an answer. Some are dead and others just don't have time to respond. Students must understand that their questions, and the subsequent answers, may differ from their peers—and that's okay!
4. If possible, read a book from a local author and invite the author to the classroom so that students can practice questioning the author with an authentic writer in the room.

Figure 26.1 Questioning the Author Prompts

Goal	Query
Initiate discussion	What is the author trying to say? What is the author's message? What is the author talking about?
Focus on author's message	That's what the author says, but what does it mean? Why did the author choose this word?
Link information	How does that connect with what the author already told us? What information has the author added here that connects or fits in with _____?
Identify difficulties with the way the author has presented information or ideas	Does that make sense? Did the author state or explain that clearly? Why or why not? What do we need to figure out or find out?
Encourage students to refer to the text because they have misinterpreted, or to help them recognize that they have made an inference	Did the author tell us that? Did the author give us the answer to that?

Source: Adapted from "Questioning the Author: A Yearlong Classroom Implementation to Engage Students with Text," by I. L. Beck, M. G. McKeown, C. Sandora, L. Kucan, and J. Worthy, 1996, *Elementary School Journal, 96,* 385–414. Published by the University of Chicago Press.

APPLICATION AND EXAMPLES

Tina Fehrang's seventh-grade English class is filled with poets. The students in this class enjoy reading and writing poetry. As part of their focus on poetry, Ms. Fehrang introduced her students to the Japanese haiku masters, including Bashō, Buson, Ikkyu, Issa, and Shiki. Using Questioning the Author, Ms. Fehrang displays several poems by Bashō on the overhead (see Figure 26.2). She reads the poems aloud and then invites her students to have a conversation about the poems.

Michael starts and asks the first question, "What is Bashō trying to say?" The conversation focuses on the life and times of this poet. The students note that Bashō must have traveled a lot to know about the different things he writes about.

Cathy asks, "Why are his poems about nature?" The discussion follows and the class decides that yes, the poems are about nature, but they don't know why. They decide to read the biography statement from one of the books in the library to find out more about this poet. They are surprised to discover that Bashō abandoned his samurai (warrior) status to become a poet.

Javier asked, "What would make you give up being a warrior? Was it too dangerous?" The class discussed this question and wondered if being a warrior had taught Bashō to look at life and nature in different ways. They hypothesized that his warrior past might have helped him get his poetry "into the hands of real people," as Andrea said.

Oliver wondered why Bashō wanted to live in a hut, rather than a large house or palace: "It's not like he couldn't afford it. He was rich, being the best poet." Again, the class discussed this question and decided that living simply allowed Bashō to stay close to nature and be able to observe his environment so that he could continue writing.

The discussion continued until Ms. Fehrang invited students to write their own haiku poems in the tradition of Bashō. As she said, "I think you know him really well, even though he lived in the middle 1600s. You have a sense of this author/poet and I'm sure you can write some amazing pieces that he would be proud of."

Figure 26.2 Haiku Poems of Bashō (1644–1694)

Along this road Goes no one, This autumn eve.	Winter seclusion: Once again I will lean against This post.	In the cicada's cry No sign can foretell How soon it must die.
	The autumn full moon. All night long I paced round the lake.	First winter rain: The monkey also seems To want a small straw cloak.

References

Beck, I. L., & McKeown, M. G. (2001). Inviting students into the pursuit of meaning. *Educational Psychology Review, 13,* 225–241.

Beck, I. L., & McKeown, M. G. (2002). Questioning the author: Making sense of social studies. *Educational Leadership, 60*(3), 44–47.

Beck, I. L., McKeown, M. G., Hamilton, R. L., & Kucan, L. (1997). *Questioning the author: An approach for enhancing student engagement with text.* Newark, DE: International Reading Association.

McKeown, M. G., & Beck, I. L. (1999). Getting the discussion started. *Educational Leadership, 57*(3), 25–28.

Literacy Focus

⬭ Before Reading	⬭ Fluency
⬭ During Reading	⬛ Comprehension
⬛ After Reading	⬭ Vocabulary
	⬭ Writing
	⬭ Oral Language

Question-Answer Relationship

The question-answer relationship (QAR) strategy is a reading strategy in which students learn to categorize comprehension questions according to where they are likely to find the answers to these questions. It is based on the three categories of question classification described by Pearson and Johnson (1978): *text explicit* (the answer is directly quoted in the text); *text implicit* (the answer must be implied from several passages in the book); and *script implicit* (requires both the text and prior knowledge and experiences).

QAR requires teachers to model the different levels of questions that are associated with a text. QAR should not be confused with Bloom's taxonomy of questions (Bloom & Krathwohl, 1956) because QAR "does not classify questions in isolation but rather by considering the reader's background knowledge and the text" (McIntosh & Draper, 1996, p. 154). In addition to serving as a tool for teachers to develop questions, it is also a framework for students to use in answering questions, even questions they face on standardized tests (Raphael & Au, 2005). QAR is a student-centered approach to questioning because it "clarifies how students can approach the task of reading texts and answering questions" (Raphael, 1986, p. 517). A comparison chart illustrating the relationship between these concepts of text questioning can be found in Figure 27.1.

STEP-BY-STEP

Question-answer relationships highlight four types of questions: Right There, Think and Search, Author and You, and On Your Own (Raphael, 1982, 1984, 1986). Because the emphasis is on understanding types of questions and where to locate the answers, students will need many exposures to all of these. It is advisable to initially teach these one at a time, so that students can deepen their understanding of each before moving on to a new type of question. Therefore, the first four steps in this procedure are not intended to be implemented in one lesson, but rather are spread out over a series of lessons. Make sure that the questions are used in conjunction with text. We find that the otherwise dry readings offered in test readiness programs can also be useful for this purpose.

1. Begin with introducing Right There questions. Explain to students that these are questions that can be answered directly from the text. These feature extended phrases from the reading in the question stem. For example, a question that reads "Who developed the first successful vaccine for polio in 1952?" would be a Right There question because a sentence in the text reads, "Jonas Salk developed the first successful vaccine for polio in 1952." Show students where these answers are located by underlining the key words and phrases.

Figure 27.1 Question-Answer Relationships

QAR strategy	Category	Description
Right There	Text explicit	The question is asked using words from the text and the answer is directly stated in the reading.
Think and Search	Text implicit	The questions are derived from the text and require the reader to look for the answer in several places and to combine the information.
Author and You	Script and text implicit	The question has the language of the text but in order to answer it the reader must use what he or she understands about the topic. The answer cannot be found directly in the text, but the text can provide some information for formulating an answer. The information is implied and the reader infers what the author meant by examining clues in the text.
On My Own	Script implicit	The question elicits an answer to come from the reader's own prior knowledge and experiences. The text may or may not be needed to answer the question.

Source: From *Improving Adolescent Literacy: Strategies at Work,* by D. Fisher and N. Frey, 2004, Upper Saddle River, NJ: Merrill/Prentice Hall. Used with permission.

2. Think and Search questions are closely related, although they differ in that the answer is assembled from more than one sentence. Let's use another polio question: "Who were the two major scientists working to develop a successful vaccine for polio?" It becomes a Think and Search question when the answer must be derived from at least two sentences: "Jonas Salk developed the first successful vaccine for polio in 1952. However, another leading researcher named Albert Sabin developed an effective polio vaccine that does not require a shot." As with Right There questions, it is helpful to underline key words and phrases for students.

3. Author and You questions are a departure from the first two because the reader plays a role in formulating answers. These questions are particularly difficult for some students because they search in vain for a "right there" answer in the text that simply doesn't exist. Author and You questions require readers to synthesize information from the text and from their own evaluation. This doesn't mean there is no correct answer. However, the correct answer must be supported by logic from the text as well as from the reader. We'll return to our polio example again. The sentences appear in an essay about the Sabin and Salk vaccines and the controversy that surrounds their research to this day. An Author and You question might look like this:

Choose the best title for this reading:

a. Polio
b. Dr. Jonas Salk
c. The Polio Vaccine and Its Controversy
d. Wiping Out a Dreaded Disease

The correct answer would be "The Polio Vaccine and Its Controversy." The other titles aren't bad, but a reader who understood the essay would choose this answer because it most closely matches the author's argument. This answer cannot be underlined in the text, but requires readers to consider the author and their own knowledge, such as the conventions of titles, to arrive at the correct answer.

4. The last type is the On Your Own question. These questions ask the reader to formulate an opinion. In theory the reader wouldn't even need to read the text if he or she possessed enough background knowledge about the topic. An example of an On Your Own question for our polio essay would be, "Do you believe that Albert Sabin deserved more credit than he has received for his work on developing a polio vaccine?" This type of question rarely appears as a multiple-choice item. Instead, it is usually tested as a short-answer or essay question.

5. Identify short text passages and questions for use in teaching QAR. As we mentioned earlier, we find test readiness materials to be useful for this because the passages are short, cover a wide range of topics, and have questions and answers prepared in advance. You may also want to look at the test generator software that accompanies your textbook. We believe strongly that work on QAR should accomplish more than one goal—namely, that it be utilized in conjunction with the content you are teaching or reviewing.

6. Prepare copies of the passages and questions for students and make another as an overhead transparency. In addition, find another short passage to use for modeling purposes. Make this into an overhead transparency as well.

7. Introduce the question and type and explain how it is located. Use the modeling passage to show students how answers are located. Use a think-aloud approach (see Strategy 43) to share your thinking about how you make choices.

8. After providing several modeled examples, distribute the student copies of the other reading. This time, invite students to take the lead in identifying and locating answers to questions. Ask them to share their thinking about how they arrived at their answers.

APPLICATION AND EXAMPLES

The preceding Step-by-Step section provides an example of how to use QAR with a specific reading. QAR helps students know where to look for an answer. Over time, students predict the location of answers based on the type of question they are reading.

Mr. Graham uses QAR regularly with his students. Over time, he releases responsibility for QAR and asks students to create questions for their readings that they can discuss with their peers. This eighth-grade social studies class is reading a collection of historical fiction related to the social studies chapter they are reading and the content standards they are studying. Following their small-group discussions about the fiction they are reading, students write QAR questions.

One group read *Sarny: A Life Remembered* by Gary Paulsen (1997). About midway through the book, the group identified the following questions:

A. Describe Sarny's courage. From whom did she gain her courage?
B. Who freed Sarny from slavery?
C. What is the difference between discipline and mistreatment?
D. Why was learning to read so important to the slaves?
E. When were slaves freed? What act freed the slaves?
F. Describe the causes of the Civil War. When and where did this war happen?

References

Bloom, B. S. & Krathwohl, D. R. (1956). *Taxonomy of educational objectives: The classification of educational goals: Handbook I, cognitive domain.* New York: Longmans.

McIntosh, M. E., & Draper, R. J. (1996). Using the question-answer relationship strategy to improve students' reading of mathematics texts. *The Clearing House, 69,* 154–162.

Paulsen, G. (1997). *Sarny: A life remembered.* New York: Delacorte Press.

Pearson, P. D., & Johnson, D. D. (1978). *Teaching reading comprehension.* New York: Holt, Rinehart and Winston.

Raphael, T. E. (1982). Teaching children question-answering strategies. *The Reading Teacher, 36,* 186–191.

Raphael, T. E. (1984). Teaching learners about sources of information for answering questions. *Journal of Reading, 27,* 303–311.

Raphael, T. E. (1986). Teaching children question-answering relationships, revisited. *The Reading Teacher, 39,* 516–522.

Raphael, T. E., & Au, K. H. (2005). QAR: Enhancing comprehension and test taking across grades and content areas. *The Reading Teacher, 59,* 206–221.

Literacy Focus	
⬭ Before Reading	⬭ Fluency
⬭ During Reading	⬛ Comprehension
⬛ After Reading	⬭ Vocabulary
	⬛ Writing
	⬭ Oral Language

RAFT Writing

Students need to "learn to write" throughout their lives. When they are in elementary school, children learn to encode words, spell, construct sentences, figure out the mechanics of paragraphs, and develop understandings of grammar. As they get older, students refine and expand on these skills. This is most commonly accomplished in the English classroom as students complete process writing pieces in which teachers comment on successive drafts of students' writing.

Writing to learn differs from other types of writing because it is not a process piece that will go through multiple refinements toward an intended final product. Instead, it is meant to be a catalyst for further learning—an opportunity for students to recall, clarify, and question what they know and what they still wonder about. In other words, writing provides students an opportunity to clarify their own thinking. Writing also provides teachers an opportunity to gauge students' understanding of content. Writing to learn "involves getting students to think about and to find the words to explain what they are learning, how they understand that learning, and what their own processes of learning involve" (Mitchell, 1996, p. 93).

Although there are a number of writing to learn prompts (e.g., Fisher & Frey, 2003), one of the most versatile is called RAFT. This prompt provides an opportunity for students to focus on perspective writing while sharing what they know about the content at hand (Santa & Havens, 1995). RAFT prompts can be written for specific books or for general topics that students are learning about. RAFT stands for:

R = role (who is the writer, what is role of the writer?)
A = audience (to whom are you writing?)
F = format (what format should the writing be in?)
T = topic (what are you writing about?)

STEP-BY-STEP

1. Based on the content that the class is studying, consider the various roles and audiences that would allow writers to consider different perspectives.
2. Vary the format for the RAFT prompt. A number of common formats are identified in Figure 28.1.
3. When students are first introduced to RAFT, everyone responds to the same prompt. For example, students may enter a geometry classroom and see the following written on the board:

R = Isosceles triangle
A = One of your angles
F = Instant messages
T = Our unequal relationship

Figure 28.1 Common Formats for RAFT Prompts

Persuasive writing	Diary entry	"Top 10" reasons
Letter	Report of information	Classified ad
Poem	Postcard	Newspaper article
E-mail	Brochure	Invitation
Instant message	Obituary	How-to manual

4. As students become increasingly familiar with writing RAFTs, vary the prompts so that different students are responding to different, but related, writing assignments. This provides them with an opportunity to discuss their responses after writing. For example, after reading the book *Starry Messenger* (Sis, 1996), students whose last name started with a letter between *A* and *M* were asked to respond to the following RAFT:

R   John Paul II
A   The world
F   Papal decree
T   The pardoning of Galileo

Students whose last name started with a letter between *N* and *Z* were asked to respond to the following RAFT:

R   Galileo
A   John Paul II
F   Letter
T   I ask for your forgiveness and understanding

APPLICATION AND EXAMPLES

U.S. history teacher Mark Seitz wanted his students to consider various perspectives of war. He wanted his students to gain an understanding and appreciation for the differing perspectives on war and the range of winners and losers in a war. He used his social studies textbook as the resource for his students to understand specific battles, the logistics, and timeline. He also used a number of picture books about wars to provide the context around these battles. Inside the front cover of each of the picture books Mr. Seitz wrote a RAFT. He asked his students to select one book per week, read it, and to respond to the RAFT. Mr. Seitz read his students' writing and wrote them back asking questions and challenging their developing ideas. Some of the books Mr. Seitz used include:

***Nim and the War Effort* (Lee, 1997)**

R   Nim
A   Teacher
F   Essay
T   My war effort

***The Wall* (Bunting, 1990)**

R   The boy
A   His grandfather
F   Letter
T   We miss you

Faithful Elephants (Tsuchiya, 1988)

R   General
A   Head zookeeper
F   Official letter
T   Ensuring the public's safety

Sadako (Coerr, 1993)

R   Sadako
A   Children of the world
F   Open letter
T   What I'm wishing for

Star of Fear, Star of Hope (Hoestlandt, 1995)

R   Lydia
A   Helen
F   Letter
T   What happened to me

References

Bunting, E. (1990). *The wall.* New York: Clarion Books.

Coerr, E. (1993). *Sadako.* New York: Putnam.

Fisher, D., & Frey, N. (2003). Writing instruction for struggling adolescent readers: A gradual release model. *Journal of Adolescent & Adult Literacy, 46,* 396–407.

Hoestlandt, J. (1995). *Star of fear, star of hope.* New York: Walker.

Lee, M. (1997). *Nim and the war effort.* New York: Frances Foster Books/Farrar, Straus and Giroux.

Mitchell, D. (1996). Writing to learn across the curriculum and the English teacher. *English Journal, 85,* 93–97.

Santa, C., & Havens, L. (1995). *Creating independence through student-owned strategies: Project CRISS.* Dubuque, IA: Kendall-Hunt.

Sis, P. (1996). *Starry messenger: A book depicting the life of a famous scientist, mathematician, astronomer, philosopher, physicist, Galileo Galilei.* New York: Farrar, Straus and Giroux.

Tsuchiya, Y. (1988). *Faithful elephants.* Boston: Houghton Mifflin.

29

Read-Alouds

Although we tend to think of teacher read-alouds as an elementary school language arts activity, there are good reasons to read aloud to middle and high school students, even across all content areas. Read-alouds allow us to show students all the ways people have written about the subjects we teach, including a range of formats, genres, and specific topics. They create a way for us to make difficult texts accessible to more students, and they provide opportunities for teachers to demonstrate the processes they use to comprehend text (Ivey, 2003). What content area teachers need to know is that teacher read-alouds help students become more engaged in the topics they teach.

Many different types of materials are appropriate for read-alouds. Some may be used to deliver important content, whereas others may be used to pique students' interest in a topic enough to read independently. It is essential to think beyond just fiction when considering the power of read-alouds. Secondary students enjoy and learn from a range of texts read by the teacher including informational books and picture books in subjects such as mathematics, art, history, science, and music, as well as poetry, popular magazine articles, newspaper items, and Internet sources.

STEP-BY-STEP

What we know about a good read-aloud, though, is that it requires thoughtful decisions. Fisher, Flood, Lapp, and Frey (2004) studied the practices of teachers who were nominated as exemplary at reading to students. An analysis across all teachers led them to suggest the following essential components of planning and carrying out a good read-aloud:

- Teachers should make good text selections.
- Teachers should preview and practice the text.
- Teachers should establish a clear purpose for listening.
- Teachers should model fluent reading.
- Teachers should read with animation and expression.
- Teachers should facilitate a discussion of the text.
- Teachers should follow up the read-aloud with student independent reading and writing.

APPLICATION AND EXAMPLES

When planning to conduct a read-aloud in any subject area, use the following principles to ensure students' comprehension and engagement:

1. *Engage student interest.* Make sure they know the purpose of your reading and that they have some idea of what it will be about before you begin. You want them to have

a reason to listen. You want to build curiosity, expectations, and anticipation in the minds of your students. For instance, you may ask students:
- Judging from the title and cover, what do you think this will be about?
- Has anybody ever heard of (the Holocaust? Circumference? Sylvia Plath?)
- What do you already know about (Abolition of slavery? Mexican culture? Concrete poems?)

2. *Read with enthusiasm.* Remember that you have an audience. Vary the intonation in your voice. Look at your students as you read. Let them know you are participating with them in experiencing the text. Share your own reactions to the text, such as:
- I'm confused by that. . .
- This is going to surprise you (shock you, disgust you, confuse you, etc.). . . .
- That is news to me. . .
- I knew that was going to happen. . .
- The author really fooled me here. . .

3. *Maintain students' engagement.* Never just read straight through the text. Stop along the way to ask prediction questions or to get students to evaluate earlier predictions they made. Share connections you are making with the text as you read. However, think twice before asking students to summarize or tell about what you just read. Ask questions and make comments that get students to anticipate upcoming text rather than to review what you just read.
- Were you right about what you thought this was going to deal with?
- Now what do you think?
- This reminds me of a documentary I just saw. . .
- This makes me think of when I. . .
- Do you remember reading about this same thing in. . .

4. *Engage students in figuring out confusing concepts and terminology.* If a new concept or term can be figured out from the context of what you're reading, show students how you do that or invite them to figure things out as you read. If a new concept or term cannot be figured out from the context, explain it to students quickly, then move on in the reading.

5. *After the reading, hold a discussion that gets them to think beyond the text.* As tempting as it is to ask recall questions to make sure students "got it," it is more useful to ask questions that get them to think more critically.
- How does this text compare to. . .
- What confused you? Surprised you? Confirmed what you believed to be true?
- Did you change your mind about anything?
- What information was left out? (Ask if you need to consult other sources. Devise a plan for future reading and research.)

References

Fisher, D., Flood, J., Lapp, D., & Frey, N. (2004). Interactive read-alouds: Is there a common set of implementation practices? *The Reading Teacher, 58,* 8–17.

Ivey, G. (2003). "The teacher makes it more explainable" and other reasons to read aloud in the intermediate grades. *The Reading Teacher, 56,* 812–814.

30

Readers' Theatre

Although Readers' Theatre has been recommended as a motivational way to increase students' reading fluency (Martinez, Roser, & Strecker, 1998), it is also excellent practice in reading for information (Young & Vardell, 1993). In Readers' Theatre, students present a text by practicing it first and then reading aloud dramatically to the whole class. Not only do students learn to read a text more fluently with each practice session, but they also revisit the information it contains, which is crucial to content area learning. By the time students read to the class, they are able to provide a clear, fluent, and thoughtful interpretation of the text, making it engaging and comprehensible to the rest of the class.

STEP-BY-STEP

Typically, texts are scripted by the teacher or small groups of students. The author's original words and phrasing are generally kept intact, but divided into meaningful parts, as in a play script. Students within small repertory groups are assigned specific parts to rehearse. Because the level of difficulty of different parts within a script can vary widely, students can be grouped by interest rather than reading level.

Scripts can be designed in interesting and useful ways. For instance, for places in this text where the author includes a key idea or main point, two or more students read at once. Also, texts that include multiple voices, such as the two writers of the letter in this Application and Examples, lend themselves to oral readings performed by multiple students. Although props can be kept to a minimum to emphasize the text itself, students might choose to present in ways that enhance the reading.

APPLICATION AND EXAMPLES

The following script was taken from a textbook. It not only addresses the role of African-American soldiers during the Civil War, but also contains a primary source, a letter written by two prospective soldiers. When performing the script below, two seventh-grade students who read the parts of the letter writers decided to remain out of the sight of the class as they read.

African-American Soldiers	
Reader 1:	Among the most eager to enlist in the Union army were free blacks in both the North and the South.
Reader 2:	Perhaps more than anyone else, they were spurred on by deeply held convictions.
Readers 1 and 2:	They believed the war could crush slavery, and so they wanted to fight for the freedom of their family and their people.
Reader 1:	They also understood that serving in the military was a cornerstone of American citizenship, and they hoped by proving themselves worthy soldiers, they might be rewarded with the full rights of citizens.
Reader 2:	Finally, they hoped that by fighting courageously, they could destroy the image many whites held of black Americans as childlike, cowardly, and untrustworthy.
Readers 1 and 2:	The United States resisted enrolling black men for a variety of reasons.
Reader 1:	Lincoln feared it would anger the Border States, who might then decide to join the Confederacy.
Reader 2:	Many white politicians recognized the same implications of military service that blacks did.
Readers 1 and 2:	It would reinforce African-Americans' claims to full citizenship and legal rights,
Reader 2:	Which they were routinely denied in the North.
Reader 1:	Eventually, the loss of white men on the battlefield, coupled with the Emancipation Proclamation of 1863, convinced Northerners of the need to enlist black soldiers.
Reader 2:	This letter to Secretary of War Simon Cameron comes from two black men in Cleveland, and represents many others that were similarly ignored by the Lincoln administration in the early part of the war.
Reader 3:	15th November, 1861
Reader 4:	Honorable Simon Cameron, Secretary of War
Reader 3:	Sir, we would humbly and respectfully state that we are colored men,
Reader 4:	Legal voters,
Reader 3:	All voted for the present administration.
Reader 4:	The question now is will you allow us the poor privilege of fighting, and, if need be, dying, to support those in office who are our own choice?
Reader 3:	We believe that a regiment of colored men can be raised in this State, who, we are sure would make as patriotic and good soldiers as any other.
Readers 3 and 4:	What we ask of you is that you give us the proper authority to raise such a regiment, and it can and shall be done.
Reader 4:	We could give you a thousand names, as either signers or references, if you required.
Reader 3:	W. T. Boyd
Reader 4:	J. T. Alston
Readers 3 and 4:	P. S. We await your reply.

Adapted from *The Civil War: A History in Documents* (*Pages for History*) (pp. 73–74), by R. G. Seidman, 2001, New York: Oxford University Press.

Some examples of other texts that are either in scripted form or are easy to script are:

Catrow, D. (2002). *We the kids: The preamble to the Constitution of the United States.* New York: Penguin Books.

Dunphy, M. (1999). *Here is the African Savannah.* New York: Hyperion Books.

Lawler, V. (1995). *I was dreaming to come to America: Memories from the Ellis Island oral history project.* New York: Puffin Books.

Maynard, M. (1999). *Micromonsters: Life under the microscope.* New York: DK.

Pappas, T. (1991). *Math talk: Mathematical ideas in poems for two voices.* San Carlos, CA: World Wide Tetra.

Winters, K. (2003). *Voices of Ancient Egypt.* Washington, DC: National Geographic.

References

Martinez, M. G., Roser, N. L., & Strecker, S. (1998). "I never thought I could be a star!" A readers theatre ticket to fluency. *The Reading Teacher, 52,* 326–337.

Young, T. A., & Vardell, S. (1993). Weaving Readers Theatre and nonfiction into the curriculum. *The Reading Teacher, 45,* 396–406

31

Literacy Focus

⬤ Before Reading		⬭ Fluency	
⬭ During Reading		⬤ Comprehension	
⬭ After Reading		⬭ Vocabulary	
		⬤ Writing	
		⬤ Oral Language	

Read-Write-Pair-Share

Read-write-pair-share is a strategy for promoting peer interaction and accountable talk to facilitate learning. This strategy is an adaptation of the think-pair-share technique first described by Lyman (1987). Students begin by reading a passage, then write a response to a prompt given by the teacher. After a few minutes, they are invited to discuss their writing with a partner. Finally, the class discusses the reading and their responses as a large group.

An advantage of using this approach is that it lowers the stakes for students who need more time to consider an idea, or who are reluctant to speak out in class. Adolescents who are English language learners may not feel comfortable speaking in class because they are insecure about their pronunciation or vocabulary. Read-write-pair-share gives them a scaffolded experience because they can first compose in writing, then discuss and expand their thoughts with one other classmate. Some may feel sure of their ideas once they have had this rehearsal and may volunteer. Even if they do not (and many students of all kinds rarely volunteer), you can be assured that everyone has been engaged and is using academic vocabulary in written and verbal forms.

We like this strategy for management purposes as well. In many classrooms, a core group of students seems to supply most of the classroom discourse. This pattern is further heightened by a teacher's desire to keep the dialogue going. Thus, teachers and students fall into a pattern where the same students engage publicly with the teacher, while the rest of the class is content to let them keep the class moving. Read-write-pair-share allows teachers to call upon a wider range of students, because each presumably has had an opportunity to write and discuss with a partner first. This is different from the "gotcha" situation good teachers strive to avoid. With read-write-pair-share, you can prompt students to read what they have written, or ask permission to read it for them. It goes without saying that if you read student writing aloud, you should read it silently first in order to understand the content and make minor adjustments to grammar and conceptual understanding.

A final advantage to this strategy is that it can be of help to girls in particular. Girls seem to answer less often in middle and high school classrooms, and there seems to be some evidence that this may be related to gender-specific concerns (Orenstein, 1995). Many girls (although certainly not all) are simply more comfortable when they have had an opportunity to check an answer with someone else first (Wilcox, Williams, & Reutzel, 1997). Read-write-pair-share can meet the needs of these students as well.

STEP-BY-STEP

1. *Read:* Students either read silently, or follow along as the teacher reads aloud.
2. *Write:* Students quickly write their impressions or reactions to the text, or answer a specific question.

3. *Pair:* Students turn to a partner and talk about what they've written.
4. *Share:* The teacher invites large-group discussion, which is much less intimidating after having just shared with a partner.

APPLICATION AND EXAMPLES

Mr. Leonardo uses read-write-pair-share as a means for introducing thought-provoking questions in his nutrition and wellness class. At the beginning of a unit on steroids, he read a newspaper article published 3 years earlier on the effects on one high school athlete. Due to use of the illegally obtained drugs, he was plagued with severe acne and sleep problems. He began losing his hair, and friendships suffered because of his mood swings. When he tested positive for anabolic steroids, he was dismissed from his school's wrestling team and lost a scholarship at the state university.

"I've just read you an article about what happened to one young man. We're going to use a strategy called read-write-pair-share," he explains. Mr. Leonardo has written the steps on the board. He describes each phase and asks them to get out a piece of paper and identify a partner.

"I'd like you to take 4 minutes to write a response to this story. If you had a chance to talk to him, what would you ask?" Mr. Leonardo walks quietly around the room while students begin to write their thoughts. A timer signals the end of the writing phase and he announces, "Take a moment to read over your writing, then talk to your partner about what you've written. Be sure to listen carefully to your partner. He or she has some good ideas, too."

Alex and Elizabeth begin a lively conversation on the fate of this athlete. "I'd be like, 'Dude, what were you thinking?'" offers Alex.

"Yeah, I know, but there are lots of guys who do it. I think he was thinking that this would give him an edge—you know, so he could get some good scholarships. That's why I wrote this question: Did you do this because of the scholarships?" Elizabeth replies.

Mr. Leonardo has been listening to conversations and is satisfied that his students have sufficiently warmed to the topic. He has noted interesting ideas and will use that information to engage some of the quieter students. "Let's wrap up your discussion and finish your thoughts," he says. He uses this verbal cue to signal students that the pair phase of the strategy is coming to a close. The class grows quieter.

"Thanks, everyone. I had a chance to listen to some great questions as I was walking around the room. Let's get some of those questions up here on the board. Take a look at what you and your partner have written."

Mr. Leonardo leads a discussion on the questions and speculations his students have about anabolic steroids. Within 10 minutes, the class has developed a list of 15 questions. Now Mr. Leonardo is ready to close this aspect of the lesson with a surprise for the class.

"Now I've got some news for you. I know the young man in this article. He attended a local high school and I met him several times during his wrestling career. He's attending another university now, and is a member of the school's wrestling team. He's also committed to doing outreach to students who may be considering, or know someone who's using, steroids. He'll be a guest speaker in our class tomorrow." The class murmurs with excitement.

You've got questions for the man. Let's get them copied down so we'll know what to ask tomorrow," Mr. Leonardo tells them.

References

Lyman, F. (1987). Think-pair-share: An expanding teaching technique. *MAA-CIE Cooperative News, 1*(1), 1–2.

Orenstein, P. (1995). *Schoolgirls: Young women, self-esteem, and the confidence gap*. New York: Random House.

Wilcox, B., Williams, L., & Reutzel, R. D. (1997). Effects of task roles on participation and productivity in the intermediate grades. *Journal of Educational Research, 51*, 344–351.

32

Literacy Focus

◯ Before Reading   ◯ Fluency
● During Reading   ● Comprehension
◯ After Reading   ● Vocabulary
           ◯ Writing
           ◯ Oral Language

Reciprocal Teaching

If teachers wish to move instruction from delivery to discovery, reciprocal teaching is an excellent choice. As an approach that allows students to directly assist with the discovery of material and the subsequent construction of meaning, the strategy is ideally suited for the classroom intent on putting learning in the hands of the learner (e.g., Little & Richards, 2000).

A review of 16 studies on reciprocal teaching suggests that this strategy increases comprehension, achievement, and standardized test scores (Rosenshine & Meister, 1994). Reciprocal teaching has also been an effective strategy for students who struggle to read (Alfassi, 1998). Finally, reciprocal teaching is a powerful strategy for consideration in multicultural classrooms, as diverse viewpoints are considered and made part of the discovery of the text (e.g., King & Parent Johnson, 1999; Palincsar & Herrenkohl, 2002).

What is reciprocal teaching and why is it so effective? Reciprocal teaching can be defined as a strategy in which students use *summarization, questioning, clarifying*, and *prediction* to help or teach each other to understand text (Palincsar, 1987; Palincsar & Brown, 1984). Definitions for each of the following can be found in Figure 32.1. Each of these four components of reciprocal teaching is based on current knowledge of comprehension instruction (e.g., Flood, Lapp, & Fisher, 2003).

STEP-BY-STEP

Reciprocal teaching highlights four comprehension processes: summarizing, questioning, clarifying, and predicting. Because the emphasis is on understanding these processes, students will need many exposures to all processes. It is advisable to initially teach them one at a time, so that students can deepen their understanding of each before moving on. Therefore, the first four steps in this procedure are not intended to be implemented in one lesson, but rather are spread out over a series of lessons.

1. Begin by introducing summarizing. Share several short readings, such as current newspaper articles, and write summary statements as a class. As students become familiar with summarizing, have them work in groups of four to read a piece of text and work on summaries of specific sections of text.
2. Follow this process for each of the remaining comprehension processes that comprise reciprocal teaching: questioning, clarifying, and predicting. It may take a few weeks for students to understand each of these tasks and the types of conversations they should have with their peers using these processes.
3. Once students understand each of the four components of reciprocal teaching, identify a reading passage or passages. Identify specific places in the text where students, in groups of four, should stop and have their reciprocal teaching conversation. Ask

Figure 32.1 Components of Reciprocal Teaching

Summarizing
- Increases comprehension through discussion.
- Builds language through interaction.

Questioning
- Focuses on main ideas of text.
- Students learn which questions provide access to information and which do not.
- Encourages higher-order questioning.

Clarifying
- Students monitor their own comprehension.
- Use peers to understand vocabulary, references to unknown events.
- Make connections to themselves, other texts, or the world.

Predicting
- Activate background knowledge.
- Determine purpose for reading.
- Make educated guess about the text.
- Serves as a motivator to confirm or disconfirm prediction.

students to take turns supplying the information to the group. For example, in his group James may summarize at the first discussion point, then question during the second, and then clarify during the third.

4. After providing several modeled examples and a few practice rounds, distribute the student copies of the other reading or readings (the entire class does not have to be reading the same thing). This time, invite students to take the lead in identifying and locating places to stop and have their reciprocal teaching conversation. Ask them to share their thinking about how they arrived at their decisions. A discussion guide for use with reciprocal teaching can be found in Figure 32.2.

APPLICATION AND EXAMPLES

Are fast-food companies responsible for the 'supersizing' of Americans?" asks Mr. McCormick. He's using a compelling reading to gain the attention of his high school health and fitness class. The reading addresses both sides of the argument, and Mr. McCormick wants them to use reciprocal teaching to discuss this controversy.

After brainstorming a list of opinions about this question, Mr. McCormick reviews the steps used in reciprocal teaching. His students have done this before, so they are familiar with the process. He has placed role cards on each table and has provided a copy of the reading for each member of the class.

Remember that your goal is to help each other understand the arguments the author uses to address both sides of this issue," he begins. "I've marked the reading at the end of each section so you'll know where to stop to discuss the reading. The role cards on the table should help if you're stuck," Mr. McCormick continues.

After counting off by fours, the students move to their groups and determine who will fulfill each role—summarizer, questioner, clarifier, and predictor. They begin to read and for several minutes the room is quiet as students learn about the changes in the American diet in the last 40 years. Soon, conversation begins.

Johnny, who is the summarizer of his group, observes that there have been important changes in the last decades, especially in the rise of obesity and Type II diabetes rates. "It says that doctors are seeing Type II in young children, which didn't used to be the case," he remarks.

Figure 32.2 Language Chart for Reciprocal Teaching

Reading: _____ Section #: _____ Date: _____

Prediction:

Question:

Clarification:

Summary Statement:

Was the prediction confirmed: YES   NO

Details:

Source: From *Improving Adolescent Literacy: Strategies at Work*, by D. Fisher and N. Frey, 2004,
Upper Saddle River, NJ: Merrill/Prentice Hall. Used with permission.

The questioner, Elisa, takes over. "I'll ask a question of all of us so we're sure we under-stand this opening section of the article. First, what's the definition of *obesity?*" Marco answers, "It's right here in the third sentence. It says, 'A person is considered obese if he or she is 30% above the ideal weight.'"

After a few more questions, the clarifier offers her input. "One thing I wondered about was the difference between Type I and Type II diabetes," says Elizabeth. "This article doesn't seem to explain it too much. I was thinking that a way to find out more about them is to look them up in the health book." A quick consultation of the glossary of their textbook explains that Type I diabetes is usually diagnosed in childhood and has a genetic link. Type II is more commonly found in adults and is related to weight, diet, and activity levels.

Now that the group has discussed aspects of the reading, they are reading to predict what information will be contained in the next passage. Rosa remarks, "Because the author has told us about the changes in the diet and health of Americans over the last 40 years, I think we're going to read about the fast-food industry. I think there will be two sides to this argu-ment; the first paragraph also mentioned that people are a lot less active these days. That's not the fault of the fast-food companies."

Mr. McCormick knows that reciprocal teaching takes time to implement, but the conver-sations that emerge are important as well. "I try to choose readings that are short but inter-esting," he says. "After all, I need to give them something to 'chew on.'"

References

Alfassi, M. (1998). Reading for meaning: The efficacy of reciprocal teaching in fostering reading comprehension in high school students in remedial reading classes. *American Educational Research Journal, 35,* 309–332.

Flood, J., Lapp, D., & Fisher, D. (2003). Reading comprehension instruction. In J. Flood, D. Lapp, J. Jensen, & J. Squire (Eds.), *Handbook of research on teaching the English language arts* (2nd ed., pp. 931–941). Mahwah, NJ: Erlbaum.

King, C. M., & Parent Johnson, L. M. (1999). Constructing meaning via reciprocal teaching. *Reading Research and Instruction, 38,* 169–186.

Little, Q., & Richards, R. T. (2000). Teaching learners—learners teaching: Using reciprocal teaching to improve comprehension strategies in challenged readers. *Reading Improvement, 37,* 190–194.

Palincsar, A. S. (1987). Reciprocal teaching: Can student discussion boost comprehension? *Instructor, 96*(5), 56–58, 60.

Palincsar, A. S., & Brown, A. L. (1984). Reciprocal teaching of comprehension-fostering and comprehension-monitoring activities. *Cognition and Instruction, 1,* 117–175.

Palincsar, A. S., & Herrenkohl, L. R. (2002). Designing collaborative learning contexts. *Theory Into Practice, 41*(1), 26–32.

Rosenshine, B., & Meister, C. (1994). Reciprocal teaching: A review of the research. *Review of Educational Research, 64,* 479–530.

33

ReQuest

ReQuest (Manzo, 1969) stands for "reciprocal questioning." ReQuest is a useful questioning technique designed to help students formulate questions and answers based on a text passage. It also gives the teacher and students opportunities to ask each other their own questions following a reading. This procedure also builds background knowledge and vocabulary through discussions and helps readers develop predictions about the reading. The goal in using ReQuest is to move students beyond low-level literal questions to higher-order thinking.

STEP-BY-STEP

ReQuest is simple to implement. The teacher chooses a passage of text, then designates short segments within the passage. A text segment can range from one sentence to an entire paragraph, based on the needs of the students.

1. The text segment is either read aloud by the teacher or read silently by both the teacher and the students.
2. When ReQuest is first being introduced, the teacher should be the one to answer questions generated by the students. During this time, the students may leave their books open, but the teacher's is closed. Students ask the teacher/respondent questions about what has been read. If students have difficult identifying questions to ask, they may need more instruction in Strategy 26, "Questioning the Author" or Strategy 27, "Question-Answer Relationship." Manzo cautions that the teacher must answer to the best of his or her ability. The students/questioners have their books open and check the teacher's answers against the text.
3. Over time, as students become familiar with the ReQuest procedure, the roles can be reversed. The students close their books, and the teacher asks the students information about the material. Then the teacher closes his or her book, and the students ask questions.
4. This procedure continues until the students have enough experience to use ReQuest with a partner. Eventually, the entire class can be divided into dyads and partnerships can read and question one another. Task cards for partners to use during the conversations can be found in Figure 33.1. At this time, the teacher can differentiate text selections so that students are not all reading the same thing, but are reading texts related to the content being studied.

Figure 33.1 ReQuest Task Cards

Questioner Task Card

1. Read the first passage silently. Pay attention to the information it contains.

2. Think of questions to ask. Try to use your own words, not exact phrases from the passage.

3. Keep your book open while you ask your question. Listen to the answer, then check to see if it is accurate. If it is not, ask another question to help the person arrive at the correct answer.

4. When finished, change roles. Repeat 2–3 times.

Respondent Task Card

1. Read the first passage silently. Pay attention to the information it contains.

2. Think of questions you might be asked. Check the passage you just read for possible answers.

3. Close your book and answer each question you are asked. You can ask the questioner to rephrase or clarify a question you do not understand.

4. When finished, change roles. Repeat 2–3 times.

APPLICATION AND EXAMPLES

The students in Mr. Andrews physics class were studying momentum. In preparation for a lab that the class would do, Mr. Andrews asked his students to find definitions of *momentum* related to science, and to use ReQuest with their partner to discuss the reading they found. Each dyad had a wireless laptop computer and began searching for interesting articles.

Tyrell and De'asia found the Wikipedia Website on momentum (*http://en.wikipedia.org/wiki/Momentum*) and began reading. Tyrell started as the questioner and asked De'asia, "What variables affect momentum?" To which she answered "mass and velocity." Tyrell then asked, "How do you define mass and velocity?" Their conversation on the opening section of the Website continued for a few minutes, then they read on.

De'asia asked, "So, how is momentum conserved?" Tyrell answered, "It says that momentum is always conserved, but I don't get that. How could that be? Hey, Mr. Andrews, can you come here?" At this point, Mr. Andrews, De'asia, and Tyrell had a conversation about conservation. When Tyrell and De'asia indicated that they "got it," they continued their reading and discussion.

During Tyrell and De'asia's conversation, other dyads were reading and discussing a wide range of other Websites that they found related to momentum. As they finished their discussions, Mr. Andrews asked his students to summarize what they knew about the scientific term *momentum* as an exit slip (see Strategy 8) and reminded them that they would begin the momentum lab the following day.

References

Manzo, A. V. (1969). The ReQuest procedure. *Journal of Reading, 13*(2), 123–126.

34

Literacy Focus

Before Reading ⬭ Fluency ⬭
During Reading ⬭ Comprehension ⬛
After Reading ⬛ Vocabulary ⬭
Writing ⬛
Oral Language ⬭

Response Writing

Many writing assignments are viewed as ways of measuring what students have learned. But we can capitalize on writing as an important component in the *process* of learning. Lots of us have had the experience of realizing new ways of thinking and new conceptualizations during and after the act of writing. We write an angry letter to a friend that we never send, and we realize that what we thought was upsetting us was not really the issue at all. We write e-mail memos to our colleagues, and then revise before we send because of additional necessary information that occurs to us as we write. As Murray (1984) puts it:

> Writing is thinking. Writing, in fact, is the most disciplined form of thinking. It allows us to be precise, to stand back and examine what we have thought, to see what our words really mean, to see if they stand up to our own critical eye, make sense, will be understood by somebody else. (p. 3)

Writing in response to any learning opportunity, be it lecture, reading, experiment, simulation, or listening activity, allows students to expand their thinking about the concepts at hand, and provides an opportunity for students to consider new information on their own. A written response differs from an oral response or a discussion because students have the chance to think without interruption, to add to their thinking, or change their thinking upon further reflection. In a sense, writing helps crystallize new knowledge.

Useful writing helps students think beyond the actual experience to which they are responding. In other words, students should be encouraged to expand, apply, or evaluate the new information rather than regurgitate it. Whereas some students may be able to write a response to an experience without any specific guidance, it is more likely the case that students will benefit from a prompt that inspires their thinking.

STEP-BY-STEP

The key to productive response writing is the understanding that there is no correct answer. Writing prompts should be crafted so that they scaffold students' thinking rather than evaluate it. Some useful ideas for creating prompts are as follows:

- Prompt students to write what was either clear or confusing to them in the learning experience.
- Have students apply new information to a new time period, place, or context.
- Ask students to compare the new information to personal experiences.
- Pose a controversial question related to the new information and have students write their opinions.
- Ask students to put themselves in the position of a key player within the event or issue at hand and write from that perspective.

APPLICATION AND EXAMPLES

Before reading aloud the picture book *Joan of Arc* (Stanley, 1998) to his class, a history teacher engaged students in a discussion on the concept of heresy, gathering background knowledge and encouraging students to keep the concept of heresy in mind as they listened. After the reading, students were asked to write using the following prompt:

In today's world who might be considered a heretic and why?

Some students wrote about specific religious or cultural groups and others posited that fewer people would be considered heretics today because of increased acceptance of different religions. One student wrote that it would depend on where a person lived.

Often, writing responses can be used as a precursor to discussion, to help students organize their thoughts and prepare to speak. For instance, in a mini-lesson on strategic reading, an 11th-grade English teacher introduced to her students the concept of "fake reading," as Tovani (2000, pp. 1–12) puts it—the act of reading the words without begin strategic and without understanding. She then asked her 11th-grade English class to read a one-page entry on The Grateful Dead from *The Book of Rock Stars: 24 Musical Icons That Shine Through History* (Krull, 2003, p. 17), knowing that this would be an engaging read for some students in the class and a challenge for others. The prompt for written response was as follows: *When you read about The Grateful Dead, were you fake reading? Why or why not?* Some students wrote that they were not fake reading, and reasoned on paper that perhaps it was due to the fact that they already knew something about The Grateful Dead or that the passage included interesting facts that kept their attention (e.g., Jerry Garcia flunked eighth grade because he refused to do homework). Others wrote that they had been guilty of fake reading because either they were country music fans, not rock and roll fans, or that there were too many words that gave them problems (e.g., *communal, pulsing*). Writing about their own experiences gave all students a chance to reflect and to become personally involved in the whole-class discussion that came later.

References

Krull, K. (2003). *The book of rock stars: 24 musical icons that shine through history*. New York: Hyperion.

Murray, D. (1984). *Writing to learn*. New York: Holt, Rinehart & Winston.

Stanley, D. (1998). *Joan of Arc*. New York: Morrow.

Tovani, C. (2000). *I read it, but I don't get it*. Portland, ME: Stenhouse.

35

Shades of Meaning

Mark Twain once said, "the difference between the right word and the almost right word is the difference between lightning and a lightning bug" (Twain, 1890). Poets certainly know this, understanding that a single "right" word is far superior to a string of "almost right" words. Accomplished writers recognize this. Any editorial columnist will tell you that the ongoing struggle of writing is to limit oneself to the essential words needed to eloquently express a position. Teachers of English language learners see this as well. Students who are learning a new language will often talk a circle around an academic term because they cannot locate the precise word.

Students in all fields of study need experiences with the terms and synonyms that describe the phenomena of the social, biological, and physical worlds. Additionally, they need to understand how these terms relate to one another. It is in the appreciation of the subtleties of these relations that an effective writer and speaker selects the right word. An effective method for introducing the relationship between words is through an activity called shades of meaning (Blanchfield, 2001). We use paint chips from the local hardware store to illustrate this idea. The variation in tint from light to dark serves as a perfect metaphor for the "shades of meaning" between and among similar words. An example of a student's list of words related to love appears in Figure 35.1.

STEP-BY-STEP

1. Ask your favorite hardware store to donate old paint chips for classroom use. Distribute these to your students as you introduce the strategy.
2. Explain that words and terms are used precisely to describe ideas, concepts, and situations. Tell students that they will experiment with expanding their understanding of the shades of meaning represented by similar terms.
3. Model shades of meaning by using a concrete example of a gradation of meaning. A continuum of temperature, light, or volume of sound work particularly well.
4. Initiate the discussion by asking for examples of the ways in which the phenomenon can be described. For instance, words associated with light include *dim, glow, bright, dazzle,* and *glaring.* You may even want to use a lamp with a dimmer switch to illustrate the range of light. List words offered by students on the board.
5. After you have garnered a number of responses, ask students to make choices about a continuum of terms. Ask them to write these terms on their paint chips.
6. Attach the paint chips to a piece of notebook paper and ask students to develop sentences using each of the terms. Ask students to write the sentences next to each block on the paint chip.

Figure 35.1 Shades of Meaning Student Sample

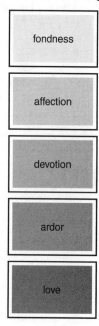

7. Explain that effective writers and speakers understand the subtle differences between related words. Ask students to work with a partner to develop other shades of meaning. Encourage them to use the thesaurus as a source of related terms.
8. The shades of meaning and example sentences can be compiled into a writer's notebook published by the class to support more effective writing.

APPLICATION AND EXAMPLES

English teacher Ms. Tariq has noticed that her sixth-grade students have acquired a habit of ineffective writing: using the same trite words as bookmarkers to explain otherwise complex ideas. Words such as *like, said,* and *nice* have peppered the journals of this writers' workshop class. She has decided to use the shades of meaning strategy to get them out of their lackluster writing habits.

"Class, I'm handing out these paint chips. Take a look at the colors on your chip and then describe them to your partner," she tells them. Within a few minutes, she is hearing terms like *turquoise* and *lime* to label colors. Other students are falling back on phrases like "orangish brown" because they lack the vocabulary to describe the color of rust.

"Some of you had trouble with this, so now I'm going to give you some help. I'm giving each group a box of 64 crayons. Each crayon has a name. Take a look at the colors on your paint chips and find names for the colors you had difficulty describing," she says.

Students quickly get down to the business of finding colors, and within a few minutes they have identified the more challenging colors.

"Your writing is like this sometimes. You get stuck for a word, and because you don't have a better one on the tip of your tongue, you use bland words like *nice* when you really should be saying something else," says Ms. Tariq. "I want you to start thinking of words as having lots of different shades of meaning, just like the crayons in the box. Sometimes you have to hunt until you find the right one. Your writer's 'crayon box' is a thesaurus."

Ms. Tariq models how the word *nice* can be better described using a range of words, such as *pleasant, polite, kind,* and *gracious.* Students write these words on another paint chip and create sentences using the words. "I'm happy to see you using the dictionary," remarks Ms. Tariq. For the remainder of the semester, Ms. Tariq requires that students turn in at least one shades of meaning paint chip with accompanying sentences each week. "It's been interesting to see the change in their writing," she said several months later. "My goal has been to develop their use of interesting and precise vocabulary in their writing. I'm not saying it's all been magically fixed by the shades of meaning activities, but I am seeing their words creeping into their general writing."

References

Blanchfield, C. (2001). *Creative vocabulary: Strategies for teaching vocabulary in K–12.* Fresno, CA: San Joaquin Writing Project.

Twain, M. (1890). In G. Bainton (Ed.), *The art of authorship: Literary reminiscences, methods of work, and advice to young beginners, personally contributed by leading authors of the day* (pp. 85–88). New York: D. Appleton.

36

Shared Reading

Two literacy practices borrowed from developmental reading theory and customized for secondary classrooms are read-alouds and shared reading. A *read-aloud* is a text or passage selected by the teacher to read publicly to a small or large group of students (see Strategy 29). A primary purpose for the read-aloud selection is to focus on the content of the text. A *shared reading* is a text or passage that is jointly shared by teacher and student, but is read aloud by the teacher. In shared readings, the students can also see the text, and it is usually chosen both for its content and as a way to draw attention to a particular text feature or comprehension strategy. In both read-alouds and shared reading, the reading is done by the teacher, not the students.

Because students can see the text in shared reading, they can associate the punctuation, layout, spacing, phrase boundaries, and other text cues used by the teacher to make decisions about how the piece should be read and interpreted. Perhaps the most powerful endorsement of this effect comes from students. A survey of 600 adolescents revealed that they attributed their literacy achievement growth to shared reading (Allen, 2001).

STEP-BY-STEP

Planning is the key to an effective shared reading. The self-assessment rubric in Figure 36.1 provides an overview of the components of an effective shared reading. The steps to plan an effective shared reading include:

1. Select a piece of text that relates to the topic under investigation.
2. Identify potential difficulties students may have with understanding the text.
3. Practice reading the text several times so that you provide a fluent model for students.
4. Identify stopping points and information you want to share with students as you are reading. The think-aloud strategy (Strategy 43) will help you plan this. Many times, you'll want to share comprehension strategies such as the ones identified in Figure 36.2, or you'll want to focus on text features such as reading maps or charts. Other times, you may want to focus on writing mechanics or literary devices such as dialogue.
5. Ensure that every student either has a copy of the text or can see the text being projected on a wall in the classroom.
6. Read aloud the text as students read along, stopping periodically to share your thinking and understandings.

APPLICATION AND EXAMPLES

During her unit of study on the American Depression, Ms. Greene wanted to vary the texts she shared with her students. She read a number of primary source documents, such as

Figure 36.1 Shared Reading Rubric for Self-Assessment

	Successfully implemented	Moderately successful	Just getting started	Not evident
Choice of text is appropriate for purpose				
Selection has been previewed and practiced				
Purpose of reading made explicit and is reflective of student needs				
Text visible to students				
Model provided of fluent reader				
Lesson design reflects scaffolding for student success				
Questions elicit thoughtful response				
Students are aware of what they are expected to do with new knowledge				
Comments:				

Source: From *Improving Adolescent Literacy: Strategies at Work,* by D. Fisher and N. Frey, 2004, Upper Saddle River, NJ: Merrill/Prentice Hall. Used with permission.

Figure 36.2 Reading Comprehension Glossary of Terms

Cause and effect—text structure used to explain the reasons and results of an event or phenomenon. Signal words for cause include *because, when, if, cause,* and *reason.* Words like *then, so, which, effect,* and *result* signal an effect.

Compare and contrast—text structure used to explain how two people, events, or phenomenon are alike and different. Some comparison signal words are *same, at the same time, like,* and *still.* Contrast signal words include *some, others, different, however, rather, yet, but,* and *or.*

Connecting—linking information in the text to personal experiences, prior knowledge, or other texts. This is commonly taught using three categories:
- ☐ Text to self: personal connections
- ☐ Text to text: connections to other books, films, etc.
- ☐ Text to world: connections to events in the past or present

Determining importance—a comprehension strategy used by readers to differentiate between essential information and interesting (but less important) details.

Evaluating—the reader makes judgments about the information being read, including its credibility, usefulness to the reader's purpose, and quality.

Inferencing—the ability to "read between the lines" to extract information not directly stated in the text. Inferencing is linked to a student's knowledge of vocabulary, content, context, recognition of clues in the text, and experiences.

Monitoring and clarifying—an ongoing process used by the reader to ensure that what is being read is also being understood. When the reader recognizes that something is unclear, he or she uses a variety of clarifying strategies, including rereading, asking questions, and seeking information from another source.

Continued

Figure 36.2 *continued*

> **Predicting**—the reader uses his or her understanding of language, content, and context to anticipate what will be read next. Prediction occurs continually during reading, but is most commonly taught as a prereading strategy.
>
> **Problem/solution**—text structure used to explain a challenge and the measures taken to address the challenge. Signal words for a problem include *trouble, challenge, puzzle, difficulty, problem, question,* or *doubt.* Authors use signal words for a solution like *answer, discovery, improve, solution, overcome, resolve, response,* or *reply.*
>
> **Question-Answer Relationships (QAR)**—question-answer relationships were developed to help readers understand where information can be located. There are four types of questions in two categories.
> 1. *In the Text*—these answers are "book" questions because they are drawn directly from the text. These are sometimes referred to as *text explicit* questions:
>   ☐ *Right There*: the answer is located in a single sentence in the text.
>   ☐ *Think and Search*: the answer is in the text but is spread across several sentences or paragraphs.
> 2. *In Your Head*—these answers are "brain" questions because the reader must generate some or all of the answer. These are sometimes called *text implicit* questions:
>   ☐ *Author and You:* the reader combines information from the text with other experiences and prior knowledge to answer the question.
>   ☐ *On Your Own:* the answer is not in the text and is based on your experiences and prior knowledge.
>
> **Questioning**—a strategy used by readers to question the text and themselves. These self-generated questions keep the reader interested and are used to seek information. Specific types of questioning includes QAR, QtA, and ReQuest.
>
> **Questioning the Author (QtA)**—an instructional activity that invites readers to formulate questions for the author of the text. The intent of this strategy is to foster critical literacy by personalizing the reading experience as they consider where the information in the textbook came from and what the author's intent, voice, and perspectives might be.
>
> **Summarizing**—the ability to condense a longer piece of text into a shorter statement. Summarizing occurs throughout a reading, not just at the end.
>
> **Synthesizing**—the reader combines new information with background knowledge to create original ideas.
>
> **Temporal sequence**—a text structure used to describe a series of events using a chronology. Signal words and phrases include *first, second, last, finally, next, then, since, soon, previously, before, after, meanwhile, at the same time,* and *at last.* Days of the week, dates, and times are also used to show a temporal sequence.
>
> **Visualizing**—a comprehension strategy used by the reader to create mental images of what is being read.

Source: From *Language Arts Workshop: Purposeful Reading and Writing Instruction,* by N. Frey and D. Fisher, 2006, Upper Saddle River, NJ: Merrill/Prentice Hall. Used with permission.

newspaper articles from this time period. She also shared published personal accounts, memoirs and diary entries, and several fictionalized accounts of this period of American history. The picture books, which were projected on the wall using a document camera, included:

- *Hannah and the Perfect Picture Pony: A Story of the Great Depression* (Zimet, 2005).
- *Children of the Dust Days* (Coombs, 2000)
- *The Babe and I* (Adler, 1999).

Ms. Greene also read a poem to her students. She wanted them to understand the perspective that many people had about the Depression—that they would "make it" in the end. As one of the poems, she selected "Life" by Paul Laurence Dunbar (see Figure 36.3).

After the first line, Ms. Greene paused and said, "What a life. I have this amazing visualization from the short line of poetry. I remember seeing the bread lines and the people sleeping

Figure 36.3 "Life," by Paul Laurence Dunbar

A crust of bread and a corner to sleep in,
A minute to smile and an hour to weep in,
A pint of joy to a peck of trouble,
And never a laugh but the moans come double;
And that is life!

A crust and a corner that love makes precious,
With a smile to warm and the tears to refresh us;
And joy seems sweeter when cares come after,
And a moan is the finest of foils for laughter;
And that is life!

Source: Poetry Alive! Retrieved from *http://www.poetryalive.com/publicdomain0203D.html*

on the streets. They were dirty, with sad looks on their face. What a picture Mr. Dunbar has given me—a crust of bread and a corner."

She continued reading through the first stanza. At the end of the first stanza, Ms. Greene paused and said, "The author has a very interesting way of talking with me. From reading this stanza, I can infer that things were pretty bad. The author describes things in relative terms—like a minute to smile but a whole hour to cry. From this, I infer that things were pretty bad, but not hopeless. There seems to be small glimpses of hope—moments of happiness or joy. I look forward to what he has to say next."

Ms. Greene read the first line of the second stanza. She paused and then reread the first line of the first stanza. She said, "Interesting. The first lines of each of the stanzas are pretty similar—yet they are different. I think that the author gives me something familiar to make a comparison and contrast the lines. The first time I read about the crust and corner, it was really sad for me, thinking about all those homeless people during the Depression. I thought that was a harsh way to start a poem. The second time I read about the corner, the happiness that I was feeling during the second stanza made me think differently about that corner. That corner is love—maybe the family lives there. What a difference."

Ms. Greene finished the poem and said, "I get it. I think that the author is saying 'that's life' you know, just deal with it. Take what you have and make the best of it. I have to think a lot about the line that joy is sweeter when cares come later. I know that I've read things with that message in them before. In fact, I think Socrates said that humans couldn't understand pleasure if they didn't also understand pain. I'm going to look up some text connections in which other people have written about balancing emotions and experience."

By modeling her thinking on a regular basis, students begin to incorporate these comprehension strategies into their reading habits. In this way, as apprentices, students begin to build their comprehension skills and develop their understanding of complex information and ideas.

References

Adler, D. A. (1999). *The Babe and I.* New York: Gulliver Books.

Allen, J. (2001). *Yellow brick roads: Shared and guided paths to independent reading 4–12.* Portland, ME: Stenhouse.

Coombs, K. M. (2000). *Children of the dust days.* New York: Carolrhoda.

Zimet, S. G. (2005). *Hannah and the perfect picture pony: A story of the Great Depression.* New York: Discovery Press.

37

Literacy Focus

⬭ Before Reading	⬭ Fluency
⬭ During Reading	⬛ Comprehension
⬛ After Reading	⬭ Vocabulary
	⬛ Writing
	⬭ Oral Language

SPAWN Writing

Writing as a vehicle for learning, reflection, and critical thinking should be used as often as possible in disciplinary classrooms (Baird, Zelin, & Ruggle, 1998; Bass, Baxter, & Glaser, 2001; Sorcinelli & Elbow, 1997). SPAWN is one way to support this kind of daily context-focused writing (Martin, Martin, & O'Brien, 1984). The *SPAWN* acronym represents five categories of prompts (see Figure 37.1). These prompts can be crafted in limitless ways to stimulate students' meaningful thinking about content area topics (Brozo, 2003). The writing prompted by SPAWN is typically short in length and can be kept in students' class notebooks or logs.

STEP-BY-STEP

1. Begin by targeting the kind of thinking students should be exhibiting. If they are to anticipate the content to be presented or reflect on what has just been learned, then certain prompts work best.
2. Select a category of SPAWN that best accommodates the kind of thinking about the content you would like students to exhibit. For example, if you would like students to regard recently learned material in unique and critical ways, the Alternative Viewpoints category prompts writing of this nature. If, on the other hand, you desire students to think in advance about an issue and brainstorm their own resolutions, the Next and Problem Solving prompts may work best.
3. Present the SPAWN prompt to students. This can be done by simply writing it on the board or projecting it from the overhead or computer. If an anticipatory prompt, students will need to see it and begin writing before the new material is presented. If a reflective prompt, it should be revealed after new content has been covered.
4. Allow students to write their responses within a reasonable period of time. In most cases prompts should be constructed in such a way that adequate responses can be made within 10 minutes. Ask students to copy the prompt in their notebooks before writing responses and record the date.
5. Because this is informal writing, SPAWN writing should not be graded as formal writing. Instead of a thorough assessment of students' SPAWN writing, most teachers who use this strategy give simple grades such as points for completing responses. We endorse this approach to evaluating SPAWN writing because we view it as a tool students can use to reflect on and increase their developing disciplinary knowledge. We would also caution against overzealous grading of structure and mechanics, which can discourage responding and critical thinking.

104

Figure 37.1 SPAWN Prompts Defined

S—Special Powers

Students are given the power to change an aspect of the text or topic. When writing, students should include what was changed, why, and the effects of the change.

P—Problem Solving

Students are asked to write solutions to problems posed or suggested by the books being read or material being studied.

A—Alternative Viewpoints

Students write about a topic or story from a unique perspective.

W—What If?

Similar to Special Powers, the teacher introduces the aspect of the topic or story that has changed, then asks students to write based on that change.

N—Next

Students are asked to write in anticipation of what the author will discuss next. In their writing, students should explain the logic of what they think will happen next.

APPLICATION AND EXAMPLES

Ulka has her history students record written responses to daily SPAWN prompts in their spiral-bound learning logs. The logs have students' personalized covers and are kept stacked on a table where they retrieve them upon entering the classroom. Each SPAWN entry is dated and labeled with the prompt given them that day. Ulka is creative in generating SPAWN prompts, presenting students with a near limitless variety of thoughtful queries. Sometimes, her students respond in their logs before the day's lesson begins to prompts requiring anticipation of the content to be covered that day:

> *Problem Solving*—We have been reading about how strong the isolationists were in the United States when World War I broke out in Europe. What do you think President Wilson could do to get their support to enter the war and help its Allies?

> *Next*—We learned yesterday that Germany has decided to use poison gas as part of trench warfare. What do you think the Allies will do next?

On other days, Ulka reserves the final 10 minutes of the class period for writing prompts that require students to reflect on or think more critically about what they have just learned:

> *Special Powers*—You have the power to change an important event leading up to the United States' entry into World War I. Describe what it is you changed, why you changed it, and the consequences of the change.

> *What If?*—What might have happened if the Turks had not entered the war on the side of the Germans?

Ulka uses Alternative Viewpoint writing to provide her students an opportunity to recall critical events in creative and interesting ways. For instance, after reading about and studying the principle causes of World War I, she wrote on the board "The Murder of Archduke Franz Ferdinand" and drew a large circle around it. She then asked the class to brainstorm all the various witnesses to the killing. Ulka drew multiple lines from the main circle and wrote as students called out. When students had exhausted all of their ideas, they were asked to select one of the persons on the board and write a description of the assassination from that perspective. The description could take on a number of forms, such as a newspaper article, a diary entry, a conversation, a letter, or just thoughts. Although Ulka told the class to be creative, she also emphasized the importance of being historically accurate.

Jon wrote a diary entry from the perspective of a man in a horse-drawn cart as it passed the duke's motorcar. Katrina described the assassination in a conversation from the vantage point of two eyewitnesses, a mother and her daughter, standing at the curbside. Peter selected a unique point of view, from the assassin himself. His learning log entry read:

> My name is Gavrilo Princip. I've been planning to commit an act of Serbian patriotism for many months. I was just waiting for the right time and place. The archduke made matters convenient for me by coming to Sarajevo. I know I will be called a terrorist, but I don't care. I am doing this to free the Serbian people from Austro-Hungarian rule. My group, the Narodna Odbrana, says murder is acceptable if it's in the name of freedom. The archduke's motorcade is approaching the sharp turn in the road now where I am waiting. His car slows down; I squeeze through a small crowd to get as close to him as I can.... I step from the curb, pull out my revolver, aim, and fire twice. Both the archduchess and archduke fall. The deed is done. Freedom is ours.

Worth noting is how Peter managed to incorporate several key historical details related to the assassination into this brief but engaging text. This text gave Peter a good reflection of his knowledge of that critical event in the history of WWI. When Ulka read it, she realized that he recalled much of the relevant information surrounding the event, such as the assassin's name, his motivations, the type of weapon used, and the location of the murder.

References

Bass, K. M., Baxter, G. P., & Glaser, R. (2001). *Using reflective writing exercises to promote writing-to-learn in science.* Paper presented at the annual meeting of the American Educational Research Association, Seattle, WA.

Baird, J. E., Zelin R. C., II, & Ruggle, L. A. (1998). Experimental evidence on the benefits of using "writing to learn" activities in accounting courses. *Issues in Accounting Education, 13,* 259–276.

Brozo, W. G. (2003). Writing to learn with SPAWN prompts. *Thinking Classroom/Peremena, 4,* 44–45.

Martin, C., Martin, M., & O'Brien, D. (1984). Spawning ideas for writing in the content areas. *Reading World, 11,* 11–15.

Sorcinelli, M., & Elbow, P. (1997). *Writing to learn: Strategies for assigning and responding to writing across the disciplines.* San Francisco: Jossey-Bass.

38

Literacy Focus

⬭ Before Reading   ⬭ Fluency
⬤ During Reading   ⬤ Comprehension
⬭ After Reading   ⬭ Vocabulary
                 ⬤ Writing
                 ⬭ Oral Language

Split-Page Notetaking

There are two main purposes of notetaking: to promote active listening and reading and to create a record for later recall and application. When students learn to take effective notes they also develop other important skills, such as the ability to summarize, paraphrase, get the gist, and differentiate between big ideas and supporting details (Boyle & Weishaar, 2001; Faber, Morris, & Lieberman, 2000).

It is critical that teachers demonstrate for students why notetaking is an important skill for them to learn (Lebauer, 2000). This can be done by reinforcing the effort–outcome connection. Students should see that when they take notes they get a payoff in the form of higher achievement (Williams & Eggert, 2002), greater understanding of information and concepts, and better performance on assignments (Titsworth & Kiewra, 2004).

One highly flexible notetaking strategy is the split-page method. As with all complex learning strategies, teachers need to model the process of taking split-page notes and structure ample time for guided practice if students are to become proficient.

Split-page notetaking has many advantages over other methods:

- The format is logically organized.
- It helps learners separate big ideas from supporting details, which promotes active listening.
- It allows for inductive and deductive prompting.

STEP-BY-STEP

1. One good way to begin teaching the split-page notetaking strategy is by showing students the difficulty of trying to study from poorly organized notes.
2. Create an example of "disorganized" notes by looking through the material to be covered and writing out main points, key terms, and specific supporting information in a mixed-up way for a section of the content. Look at the example in Figure 38.1. Notice when trying to study and recall the material how confusing it would be to sort out the important from the less important with a random notetaking scheme like that. An example can be given to students in a handout, presented as an overhead, or shown on a computer slide.
3. Present another section of the material to be covered in the split-page format (see examples of split-page notes in Figures 38.2, 38.3, and 38.4). Do this by drawing a straight line from top to bottom on a piece of paper (preferably a sheet of normal-sized, lined notebook paper) approximately 2 to 3 inches from the left edge. Try to split the page into one third and two thirds.

Figure 38.1 Example of Disorganized Notes

1. light = Radiant energy
    Autotropic—make own food—Producer
    Heterotropic—cannot make own food
    Energy-kinetic (moving), potential (storage)
    Radiant-(heat, light)
  Enzymes = catalyst Coenzymes
    work with enzymes
    work as transfer agents-products from enzyme reaction
    made up of vitamins
    unspecific—will work with many enzymes

Figure 38.2 Split-Page Notes for English Class

"The Most Dangerous Game"—Richard Connell

February 12, 2007

English 10, 3rd Block

Plot defined	related events that present and resolve a problem/conflict
Rainsford Sanger	celebrated hunter forced to become hunted
Setting	Ship Trap island Caribbean Sea jungle environment General Zaroff's preserve
Plot	R. falls overboard R. swims to shore Zaroff admits to hunting men Zaroff hunts R.

Figure 38.3 Split-Page Notes for Business Education Class

Unemployment and Inflation

September 22, 2007

5th period

Full employment of the labor force	Everyone who can and wants to work is working Incentives for employers and labor to choose unemployment over lowered wages
Who are unemployed?	Highest among teenagers, minorities, unskilled Blacks 2 x that of whites Higher for women than men
Measures of inflation	Consumer Price Index (CPI) By Dept. of Labor Reflects prices of goods/services Wholesale Price Index (WPI)

4. In the left column write big ideas, key dates, names, and so on. Write supporting information in the right column. Paraphrase and abbreviate as much as possible (see Figures 38.2, 38.3, and 38.4).
5. Discuss the advantages of taking notes in this way. Show students how they can prompt recall by bending the sheet so that information in the right or left columns is covered.

Figure 38.4 Split-Page Notes for Geology Class

Chapter 11, Metallurgy	October 4, 2007
Metallurgy	taking metals from ore —refining ores —preparing ores
Ores	—rock or mineral —metal obtained profitably
Metallurgy of iron	
Iron Age	—began 1500 BC —5000 BC meteorites were used
Iron	—4th most abundant —reddish brown
Taconite	—found @ Lake Superior —25%–50% iron —crushed/refined

6. Present another section of the material while students attempt to take split-page notes on their own. In advance, prepare a model of the information in split-page format and compare your organization of the content with students' attempts.
7. Continue to guide students in the process of taking split-page notes by modeling the format with notes of the content and eliciting similar-styled notes from students. Undoubtedly, it will take time for students to become comfortable with the format and develop their own individual nuances within the split-page structure. This guided practice time will be well spent because it's the best way to ensure students learn and take full advantage of the notetaking system.

APPLICATION AND EXAMPLES

Figures 38.2 through 38.4 show three examples of split-page notes taken by students for a novel in English, a lecture in business, and a chapter on geology in science. Notice how each one follows the overall format of the split-page scheme yet incorporates small variations. As noted, students should be encouraged to individualize and personalize split-page notes once they become fluent with the strategy. This promotes a sense of ownership, which increases the likelihood students will retain the notetaking habit.

References

Boyle, J. R., & Weishaar, M. (2001). The effects of strategic note-taking on the recall and comprehension of lecture information for high school students with learning disabilities. *Learning Disabilities: Research & Practice, 16*, 133–141.

Faber, J. E., Morris, J. D., & Lieberman, M. G. (2000). The effect of note taking on ninth grade students' comprehension. *Reading Psychology, 21*, 257–270.

Lebauer, R. S. (2000). *Learn to listen: Listen to learn. Academic listening and note-taking* (2nd ed.). New York: Longman.

Titsworth, B. S., & Kiewra, K. A. (2004). Spoken organizational lecture cues and student note-taking as facilitators of student learning. *Contemporary Educational Psychology, 29*, 447–461.

Williams, R. L., & Eggert, A. (2002). Note-taking predictors of test performance. *Teaching of Psychology, 29*, 234–237.

39

Literacy Focus

- ⬭ Before Reading
- ⬭ During Reading
- ⬛ After Reading

- ⬭ Fluency
- ⬛ Comprehension
- ⬭ Vocabulary
- ⬭ Writing
- ⬛ Oral Language

Student Booktalks

Adults would seldom choose to read a book without some sort of preview or hook to grab their attention. When visiting a large bookstore, for instance, it is difficult to decide on a purchase without an idea of what might be good to read. For inexperienced middle and high school readers, and particularly in content area subjects, it makes sense to have regular opportunities for student booktalks. The sharing of books serves two important purposes. First, it allows readers to express their opinions and offer personal responses to the books they have selected. Second, it gives peers an opportunity to identify books they might like to try on their own.

For fiction books, the booktalk serves as a lure to attract otherwise uninterested readers. Donelson and Nilson (1997) suggest that "booktalks are comparable to movie previews or teasers presenting the characters and a hint of the plot, but they never reveal the ending" (p. 302). For nonfiction texts, the booktalk can serve as a way to present the range of books available on a certain topic, but also to show students what might be interesting about a new or unfamiliar topic.

STEP-BY-STEP

The regular modeling of booktalks by the teacher is both helpful and necessary. The following guidelines can be used to aid students in preparing and presenting useful booktalks:

- Bring the book to show as you talk about it.
- Keep the booktalk brief, generally no more than about 3 to 4 minutes.
- Do not tell too much about the book. Your goal is to get others to read.
- For fictional stories, tell the topic and something about the story, but do not tell the plot. Feature a scene or character the story revolves around, but do not give away the ending.
- For nonfiction texts, tell or show something from the book that would make people more interested in the topic of the book. Focus on intriguing but important details.
- Feature a short excerpt from the book.
- Compare the book to similar books or others by the same author.

APPLICATION AND EXAMPLES

Consider the following comments made by a student who read *Exploding Ants: Amazing Facts About How Animals Adapt* (Settel, 1999):

> The things animals do can be really gross, like I learned that tongue worms eat dog mucus, and vampire bats eat blood that gets vomited by other bats.

Figure 39.1 Planning Student Booktalks

Monday	
25 minutes:	Teacher read-aloud(s) and booktalks
	This is a time to introduce materials and get students familiar with the kinds of things they will have the opportunity to read during this period.
15 minutes:	Student browsing/reading of available books

Tuesday	
10 minutes:	More teacher read-aloud(s) and booktalks
5 minutes:	Introduction of reading logs
15 minutes:	Students read books of choice
10 minutes:	Students complete reading log

Wednesday	
10 minutes:	More teacher read-aloud(s) and booktalks
25 minutes:	Students read books of choice
5 minutes:	Students complete reading log

Thursday	
10 minutes:	Teacher presents one booktalk and explains to students how to prepare a short booktalk. (e.g., using information they've written in their logs about certain books, sharing a favorite quote, telling why a person should read that book, etc.). This is in preparation for Friday's class.
20 minutes:	Students read books of choice
10 minutes:	Students complete reading log and select something they have read for a booktalk to be presented on Friday

Friday	
40 minutes:	Student booktalks (any leftover time could be used for reading or teacher read-alouds)

Of course, these details caused several of his classmates to grab for the book immediately following the sharing time.

There are several places in the school day where students could benefit from peer booktalks. First, in a language arts or English classroom that offers regular times for independent reading or a workshop-type instructional framework or as part of a schoolwide independent reading time, booktalks can be used to inspire and motivate student book selection. Figure 39.1 contains a sample scenario of how booktalks could be introduced into a 40-minute reading workshop or independent reading program.

In other content area classes where informational texts may be more prominent than fiction, booktalks can be useful as students are engaged in independent, paired, and small-group inquiry projects that require in-depth reading. When students become experts on particular topics through inquiry, they can also be seen as experts on the texts pertaining to those topics.

References

Donelson, K. L., & Nilson, A. P. (1997). *Literature for today's young adults* (5th ed.). New York: Longman.

Settel, J. (1999). *Exploding ants: Amazing facts about how animals adapt.* New York: Atheneum.

40

Literacy Focus

- ⬛ Before Reading
- ⬜ During Reading
- ⬜ After Reading
- ⬜ Fluency
- ⬛ Comprehension
- ⬛ Vocabulary
- ⬜ Writing
- ⬜ Oral Language

Student Questions for Purposeful Learning

All middle and high school teachers hope to develop students' abilities to read, listen, and learn with a purpose. Purposeful learning is associated with higher levels of engagement and achievement (Ediger & Pavlik, 1999; Schunk & Zimmerman, 1998). It leads to focused and sustained attention (Guthrie & Wigfield, 2000), and it enlivens classroom lessons. Student questions for purposeful learning, or SQPL, is a strategy designed to gain and hold students' interest in the material by having them ask and answer their own questions. When students instead of the teacher or text pose questions about what is to be learned, they become much more motivated to pay close attention to the information source for answers to their questions. Although SQPL begins with a teacher prompt to stimulate student questions, the process can become internalized so that students can begin to ask and answer questions on their own over content they must learn. SQPL legitimizes students' own questions as vehicles for learning. Instead of being interrogated, they become interrogators exploring information and ideas with purpose and with heightened attention.

STEP-BY-STEP

The steps involved in an SQPL lesson are as follows:

1. Look over the material to be read and covered in the day's lesson. Think up a statement related to the material that would cause students to wonder, challenge, and question. The statement does not have to be factually true as long as it provokes interest and curiosity. See Figure 40.1 for examples of question-provoking statements for various disciplinary topics.
2. Present the statement to students. Most often teachers write the statement on the board, though it can also be projected on the overhead or from a computer, put on a handout, and even stated orally for students to record in their notebooks.
3. Have students pair up and, based on the statement, generate two or three questions they would like answered. The questions must be related to the statement and should not be purposely farfetched or parodies.
4. When all student pairs have thought of their questions, ask someone from each team to share questions with the whole class.
5. As students ask their questions aloud, write them on the board. Eventually, similar questions will be asked by more than one pair. These should be starred or highlighted in some way.

Figure 40.1 Sample SQPL Question-Provoking Statements
for Disciplinary Topics

English

Topic: Courtroom chapters in *To Kill a Mockingbird*
SQPL Statement: *Atticus is wasting his time defending Tom.*

Math

Topic: Measuring three-dimensional objects
SQPL Statement: *With just a ruler I can tell you the total distance around the Earth.*

History

Topic: Communism in post-WWII Europe
SQPL Statement: *People are happiest when government takes care of all their needs, and everyone is equal.*

---

6. Once all questions have been shared, look over the student-generated list and decide whether you need to add some questions of your own. This may be necessary when students have failed to ask about important information you want to be sure they learn. Tell students you thought up some questions, too, and would like to add them to the list.
7. At this point, students will be ready for the information source so they can seek answers to their questions. Tell them as they read or listen to pay attention to information that helps answer a question from the board. They should be especially focused on material related to the questions that were starred. These might be considered class consensus questions.
8. As content is covered, stop periodically and have students discuss with their partners which questions could be answered; then ask for volunteers to share.
9. Students might be required to record the questions from the board and the answers they find in their notebooks for later study.

APPLICATION AND EXAMPLES

> *It's only a matter of time before Earth*
> *will be hit by a large object from outer space.*

A seventh-grade science teacher wrote these words on the board for his class. He then asked his students to find a partner and think of three questions they would like answered about this statement. The teacher knew he had piqued curiosity when even his most reluctant student began talking excitedly about the explosion such a calamitous event would cause. Afterward, he gathered questions from the class and wrote them on the board. He placed a star next to the ones that were similar in order to highlight common themes of interest among class members. For example, several pairs of students wanted to know what kind of object would strike Earth; many others were interested in finding out what would happen as a result of such a collision; still others asked whether an object could be stopped. Once all students' questions were solicited they were eager to have answers.

At this stage, the students were ready for the presentation of the information. SQPL is adaptable to virtually any information source—such as lecture, discussion, video, the Internet, and printed text—the science teacher used. He told the class to read the section in their science books about asteroids, searching for answers to their own questions and recording them in their notebooks. He stopped the class periodically to discuss answers to students' questions.

The teacher has found that even when he demands students' attention, he's never completely sure they are doing so because it is so easy to create the illusion of attentiveness. His students are more likely to pay attention to the reading material, lectures, and other information sources in class when they are brought into the flow of instruction with engaging learning strategies. SQPL is one of several ways he accomplishes this. By striving to maximize student engagement and expand meaningful learning the teacher finds less mock participation and more genuine attentiveness.

References

Ediger, A., & Pavlik, C. (1999). *Reading connections: Skills and strategies for purposeful reading.* New York: Oxford University Press.

Guthrie J., & Wigfield, A. (2000). Engagement and motivation in reading. In M. Kamil, P. Mosenthal, P. D. Pearson, & R. Barr (2002), *Handbook of reading research* (Vol. 3, pp. 403–422). Mahwah, NJ: Erlbaum.

Schunk, D. H., & Zimmerman, B. J. (1998). *Self-regulated learning from teaching to self-reflective practice.* New York: Guilford Press.

41

Literacy Focus

⬤ Before Reading   ⬭ Fluency
⬭ During Reading   ⬤ Comprehension
⬭ After Reading   ⬭ Vocabulary
           ⬭ Writing
           ⬭ Oral Language

Text Impressions

This readiness strategy creates a situational interest in the content to be covered by capitalizing on students' curiosity. By asking students to form a written or oral impression of the topic to be discussed or text to be read, they become eager to discover how closely their impression matches the actual content (Brozo, 2004). The strategy may not automatically engender an overall and long-lasting appeal for the topic, but helps keep youth focused and engaged at a particular point in time and in a given setting, or least during the timeframe of the lesson. This is what we mean by situational interest. This "impressions" strategy can also be used before students encounter any information source, including a textbook or tradebook chapter, a lecture, a guest speaker, a DVD, a WebQuest, a field trip, and so on. For that reason, it's a versatile strategy that can increase motivation by heightening anticipation and providing a meaningful purpose for learning (Guthrie & Humenick, 2004).

STEP-BY-STEP

The basic process of conducting a lesson impression is:

1. Review the material for the day's lesson and select several key terms students will read or hear. Nouns and verbs work best and sometimes it's appropriate to include two, or three, word phrases, such as "cold spring" or "crash landing."
2. From the initial long list of words, identify a smaller number of them that stand out as suitable for leaving students with a pretty good impression but not a complete picture of the content.
3. Present the smaller list of the ideal words to students. This can be done in a number of ways. Words can be written or projected on the board, given in handout form, or even spoken for students to write in their notebooks. Words should be presented in the order in which students will encounter them in the lesson.
4. Tell students they are to use the words to make a guess as to what will be covered in class that day. Depending on the nature of the content, students should be encouraged to write a short descriptive passage, a story, or an essay. Be sure to remind students they are to use every word in their impression writing. Tell the students they do not have to use the words in their writing in the same order in which they received them.
5. Allow a reasonable amount of time for students to complete the writing while monitoring their progress and clarifying the task.
6. When students finish their short compositions, invite volunteers to read what they have written to the class. Anticipation is heightened when several students share their different impressions, leaving the class wondering whose impression is closest to the actual content.

7. Present the content. Students will read or listen closely to compare their impression writing with the text, lecture, or other information source. To help students keep track of the similarities and differences, they can be asked to make a Venn diagram. In one circle they can list their ideas; in the other, the actual information; and in the overlapping space, the common ideas.

APPLICATION AND EXAMPLES

Teachers from every discipline can use the lesson impression strategy to increase motivation and help students focus more closely on the content of any given lesson. For example, an 11th-grade English teacher employed the strategy as a prelude to reading Franz Kafka's *The Metamorphosis*.

First, she began by presenting her students with a list of words and phrases taken directly from the story content about to be read. For example, the following words were written on the board:

Gregor
sleep
morning
insect
sister
fear

Next, she asked the students to write a story or description that included these words. The idea behind this strategy is that the words give just an impression of the initial plot action in the story, leaving students to try to fill in the gaps with their hunches, guesses, and creative imaginations. She allowed any student who had difficulty writing his or her own impression story to team up with a classmate and dictate a story. When finished writing, volunteers were asked to read their stories aloud and lead the class in a discussion about the similarities and differences among them. One student's text read:

> There once lived an unhappy man named Gregor. He was unhappy because every night while he would sleep, an insect would sting him. One morning he woke up and his sister saw that he had a big red sore from an insect bite. She was filled with fear and took him to the doctor right away.

A team of two students crafted the following piece:

> Gregor loved insects. He took long walks in the forest just to look at them. In his sleep he dreamt about them. One morning he left for the forest and didn't return by the end of the day. His sister called the police out of fear that something had happened to Gregor. The next day when the police found him they learned he had gotten lost following a beautiful butterfly.

After a variety of impressions were shared, the class was eager to discover which one was the most accurate. At this point, she passed around paperback copies of the novella and read the opening of the *The Metamorphosis* aloud as students followed along in their books. While reading she asked students to listen to how closely their impression stories matched the events of the actual story.

The teacher has noticed how the lesson impression strategy helps her students become more engaged listeners and readers. As their attention to story content increases, their comprehension and retention improves as well.

References

Brozo, W. G. (2004). Gaining and keeping students' attention. *Thinking Classroom/Peremena, 5*, 38–39.

Guthrie, J. T., & Humenick, N. M. (2004). Motivating students to read: Evidence for classroom practices that increase reading motivation and achievement. In P. McCardle & V. Chhabra (Eds.), *The voice of evidence in reading research* (pp. 329–354). Baltimore: Brookes.

Kafka, F. (1993). *The metamorphosis and other stories* (translated by Joachim Neugroschel). New York: Charles Scribner's Sons.

42

Text Structures

In content area classrooms, students are expected to read for information. These informational, expository, or nonfiction texts commonly use text structures to convey content. Text structures are the organizational arrangements writers use to present information. Common text structures include:

- *Descriptive*—these texts provide rich details about people, places, and phenomena.
- *Compare and contrast*—these texts provide readers with information about how two things are like and different.
- *Cause and effect*—these texts describe the causal relationships between phenomena.
- *Problem/solution*—these texts identify a problem and how the problem was solved. They are a bit more complex because the problem and solution discussion may occur over several paragraphs or pages.
- *Temporal sequence*—these texts describe events in a sequence, often in chronological order.

In addition to the text structure, informational texts also contain a number of visual markers. These visual markers may be used to show a sequence (e.g., dates, numbers, a timeline) or a comparison (e.g., a table, matrix, or columns). Text structures are often recognized by the specific key words and phrases that signal their presence (e.g., "first, second, . . ." or "as a result . . ."). Figure 42.1 contains a list of common signal words. Texts that are constructed according to common text structures are easier to read, understand, and remember (Dymock, 2005; Moss, 2004). As students become familiar with common text structures, their writing improves as they implement these conventions.

STEP-BY-STEP

Students need to be taught about text structures and then be expected to use these structures in their reading comprehension and writing. To introduce text structures, use the following process. As students become familiar with the process, ask them to incorporate these procedures into their habits.

1. *Survey the text.* Model skimming and scanning the text to note the organization of the text and the use of features such as tables, graphics, headings, and so forth.
2. *Identify signal words.* As you skim and scan the text, note the use of signal words (see Figure 42.1). You may want to underline the signal words or use a sticky note to identify these clues to the text's organization.
3. *Determine the text structure.* Based on the organization and the use of signal words, identify the text structure being used. Note that different paragraphs may use different structures, but that understanding the structure helps readers process information.

Figure 42.1 Key Words Found in Text Structures

Description	*Lots of adjectives and details:* for example, involves, specifically, can be defined, for instance, in particular, on, over, next to, also, within
Compare and contrast	different from, same as, alike, like, similar to, unlike, in comparison, in common, as well as, as opposed to, yet, different from, either . . . or, not only . . . but also, whereas, although, most, however, on the other hand, opposite, opposed to, otherwise, still, while, although
Cause and effect	because, so that, thus, unless, therefore, since, in order to, as a result of, effects of, if . . . then, this led to, leads to, then, reasons for, then . . . so, for this reason, consequently, an explanation for, when . . . then
Problem/solution	problem is, a solution is, solved by, alternative, possible answer, therefore, conclusion, evidence is, a reason for
Temporal sequence	to begin with, after, afterward, not long after, first, second, in addition, on (date), before, during, initially, next, then, last, additionally, finally, another, also, earlier, later, meanwhile, today, when

4. *Organize a notetaking tool.* Based on the text structure, invite students to identify a notetaking tool that they could use to record information from their reading. This could involve concept maps (Strategy 3), pattern guides (Strategy 22), or split-page notetaking (Strategy 38).
5. *Predict the main idea.* Based on the purpose for reading and the text structures being used, predict the main idea of the passage. Making this prediction helps readers use their knowledge of print and how print works. It also helps readers establish a purpose for reading.
6. *Read the text and take notes.* At this point, the reader is ready to read for information.

APPLICATION AND EXAMPLES

Biology teacher Jeff Johnson wants to ensure that his students use information about text structures to understand scientific information. Mr. Johnson regularly reads aloud to his students (Strategies 29 and 36) and thinks aloud about the text (Strategy 43) as they read along. He likes to project a text from the Internet using his LCD data projector. One of his favorite sites is Science Daily *(http://www.sciencedaily.com).*

Mr. Johnson regularly starts his shared reading events to talk with students about the text structure. For example, Mr. Johnson scanned an article about the scientists' discoveries of the castor bean. In doing so, he noted paragraphs that were rich in descriptions and compared those paragraphs to those that used a temporal sequence structure to explain the chronology of thinking about the usefulness of the castor bean and its oil.

Following this discussion of the text structures and his shared reading, Mr. Johnson asked his students to use their laptops as research tools to investigate the structure of plants. He reminded his students to organize their notes after they had found an article or Website in which plant structures were discussed, and to be sure they skimmed and scanned the text in advance to ensure that their selection matched the purpose, was readable, and that they understood the text structure being used by the writer. Because they were novices in using and understanding text structure, Mr. Johnson provided his students with a reading research tool to guide their thinking about text structures (see Figure 42.2). Once his students become familiar with text structures and establishing purposes for their independent reading, he will discontinue the use of this tool.

As Mr. Johnson says, "I have a lot of work to do to ensure that my students think like scientists. They need to read texts related to our class investigation, but they need to know how to find texts that are interesting and that they can read. They also need tools to read these texts and help with understanding the structures of these texts."

Figure 42.2 Reading Research Tool

Answer the following questions *before* you read the text:

A. Survey the text—what features are used to help you understand the information?

B. Scan the text—what is the purpose?

C. Scan the text—which signal words are used?

D. Consider the text—which text structures are used?

E. Analyze the text—what is the main idea (or ideas)? Is this consistent with your purpose for reading?

F. Plan for reading—which tool will you use to take notes from the text?

Now you're ready to read!

References

Dymock, S. (2005). Teaching expository *text* structure awareness. *The Reading Teacher, 59*, 177–181.
Moss, B. (2004). Teaching expository text structures through information trade book retellings. *The Reading Teacher, 57*, 710–718.

43

Literacy Focus

● Before Reading	○ Fluency
○ During Reading	● Comprehension
○ After Reading	● Vocabulary
	○ Writing
	○ Oral Language

Think-Alouds

Certain aspects of reading are very observable. For instance, you know when readers sound fluent, read with expression, and read words accurately. However, other important dimensions of reading cannot be seen or heard. When you are reading silently, you are employing a multitude of skills and strategies that even you may be unaware that you are using to make sense of the text. For instance, productive readers ask themselves questions, monitor their understanding of what they are reading, take measures to fix their comprehension when it breaks down, create visual images of what they are reading, draw inferences, and make connections between the text they are reading and other things they know or have experienced. It is not surprising that all of these processes contribute greatly to comprehension.

Surely, some students figure out these processes on their own, whereas other students need these productive behaviors modeled and explained. Even otherwise successful readers may need reminders to be strategic when reading new or unfamiliar texts in a range of subject areas. One way for teachers to make the reading process more observable to students is through thinking aloud as they read to students. In short, teachers read a portion of text and then stop, step aside from the text, and verbalize what they are doing to make sense of the text. A list of common comprehension strategies teachers use when thinking aloud can be found in Figure 43.1. What the think-aloud accomplishes is teaching students that productive reading is not passive; the reader can consciously and deliberately negotiate his or her understanding of a text.

STEP-BY-STEP

Duffy, Roehler, and Herrmann (1988) offer the following four suggestions for considering think-alouds:

- Present the strategy in real text (not in workbooks or texts created for skills teaching).
- Describe the mental acts readers employ during productive reading as a way of equipping students with the knowledge necessary to take control of their own cognitive processes.
- Provide examples and nonexamples that demonstrate the goal of flexible thinking.
- Combine modeling with opportunities to express their own thinking while reading.

Figure 43.1 Reading Comprehension Glossary of Terms

Cause and effect—text structure used to explain the reasons and results of an event or phenomenon. Signal words for cause include *because, when, if, cause,* and *reason.* Words like *then, so, which, effect,* and *result* signal an effect.

Compare and contrast—text structure used to explain how two people, events, or phenomenon are alike and different. Some comparison signal words are *same, at the same time, like,* and *still.* Contrast signal words include *some, others, different, however, rather, yet, but,* and *or.*

Connecting—linking information in the text to personal experiences, prior knowledge, or other texts. This is commonly taught using three categories:
- ☐ Text to self: personal connections
- ☐ Text to text: connections to other books, films, etc.
- ☐ Text to world: connections to events in the past or present

Determining importance—a comprehension strategy used by readers to differentiate between essential information and interesting (but less important) details.

Evaluating—the reader makes judgments about the information being read, including its credibility, usefulness to the reader's purpose, and quality.

Inferencing—the ability to "read between the lines" to extract information not directly stated in the text. Inferencing is linked to a student's knowledge of vocabulary, content, context, recognition of clues in the text, and experiences.

Monitoring and clarifying—an ongoing process used by the reader to ensure that what is being read is also being understood. When the reader recognizes that something is unclear, he or she uses a variety of clarifying strategies, including rereading, asking questions, and seeking information from another source.

Predicting—the reader uses his or her understanding of language, content, and context to anticipate what will be read next. Prediction occurs continually during reading, but is most commonly taught as a prereading strategy.

Problem/solution—text structure used to explain a challenge and the measures taken to address the challenge. Signal words for a problem include *trouble, challenge, puzzle, difficulty, problem, question,* or *doubt.* Authors use signal words for a solution like *answer, discovery, improve, solution, overcome, resolve, response,* or *reply.*

Question-Answer Relationships (QAR)—Question-answer relationships were developed to help readers understand where information can be located. There are four types of questions in two categories.
1. In the Text—these answers are "book" questions because they are drawn directly from the text. These are sometimes referred to as text explicit questions:
   - ☐ Right There: the answer is located in a single sentence in the text.
   - ☐ Think and Search: the answer is in the text but is spread across several sentences or paragraphs.
2. In Your Head: these answers are "brain" questions because the reader must generate some or all of the answer. These are sometimes called text implicit questions:
   - ☐ Author and You: the reader combines information from the text with other experiences and prior knowledge to answer the question.
   - ☐ On Your Own: the answer is not in the text and is based on your experiences and prior knowledge.

Questioning—a strategy used by readers to question the text and themselves. These self-generated questions keep the reader interested and are used to seek information. Specific types of questioning includes QAR, QtA, and ReQuest.

Questioning the Author (QtA)—an instructional activity that invites readers to formulate questions for the author of the text. The intent of this strategy is to foster critical literacy by personalizing the reading experience as they consider where the information in the textbook came from and what the author's intent, voice, and perspectives might be.

Synthesizing—the reader combines new information with background knowledge to create original ideas.

Summarizing—the ability to condense a longer piece of text into a shorter statement. Summarizing occurs throughout a reading, not just at the end.

Temporal sequence—a text structure used to describe a series of events using a chronology. Signal words and phrases include *first, second, last, finally, next, then, since, soon, previously, before, after, meanwhile, at the same time,* and *at last.* Days of the week, dates, and times are also used to show a temporal sequence.

Visualizing—a comprehension strategy used by the reader to create mental images of what is being read.

Source: From *Language Arts Workshop: Purposeful Reading and Writing Instruction,* by N. Frey and D. Fisher, 2006, Upper Saddle River, NJ: Merrill/Prentice Hall. Used with permission.

APPLICATION AND EXAMPLES

Consider the following excerpts from a think-aloud. Here a science teacher begins reading from *Supercroc and the Origin of Crocodiles* (Sloan, 2002, p. 6):

Teacher (to class): I'm going to think aloud as I read to show you how I try to understand the information I read in science books. I'll let you know when I'm confused, what I do to clear up my confusion, how I predict what the author might say, what pictures turn up in my mind as I read, and other things I do in my head.

Teacher (reading): *In the middle of the Ténéré desert, whose name means "nothing," are crocs of all sizes. Among them is Supercroc—one of the biggest types of croc ever to have lived on earth.*

Teacher (to class): I'm already confused. I've never heard of crocodiles living in the desert. I thought they lived in water. I'll have to keep reading to see if there are crocodiles that live in deserts or if I just misunderstood.

Teacher (reading): *Once crocs swam here in deep rivers and lakes that cut across a forested plain, but now they are just bones that lie scattered in the sand of this sub-Saharan desert of Niger.*

Teacher (to class): Now I get it. This used to be water, and over time it became a desert. I predict that the crocodile bones are fossils. I'm going to keep reading to find out.

Notice that this teacher does not provide a list of instructions or procedures for comprehending. Duffy and colleagues (1998) remind us that strategic reading cannot be summed up in a linear set of steps, but instead that readers must adapt and be flexible depending upon the text itself or the purpose of the reading. For this reason, it is also clear that a single lesson that involves mental modeling may not have much of an effect on students' reading. Students need to see how good readers process information in a variety of texts. For instance, what goes on in a person's head when they read a historical document? How do you negotiate your way through a scientific journal? Likewise, students need to understand strategies for a host of situations created by the texts they read. For example, some texts contain new or unfamiliar vocabulary, and it may be that inexperienced readers do not know that oftentimes the sentences surrounding the new term give clues for its definition. Also, a certain kind of text may evoke strong visual images that help a person comprehend. Chances are, if a teacher is using a wide range of texts in teaching students about a topic, then many opportunities to model strategic processes will arise.

References

Duffy, G. G., Roehler, L., & Herrmann, B. A. (1988). Modeling mental processes helps poor readers become more strategic. *The Reading Teacher, 41,* 762–767.

Sloan, C. (2002). *Supercroc and the origin of crocodiles.* Washington, DC: National Geographic.

44

Literacy Focus

◯ Before Reading   ◯ Fluency
◯ During Reading   ◯ Comprehension
⬤ After Reading   ⬤ Vocabulary
                              ◯ Writing
                              ◯ Oral Language

Tossed Terms

Tossed terms is a strategy that can be used to review ideas before a test or as a way to help students acquire essential vocabulary. It is a generative strategy in that students prompt and clarify for one another newly learned information and ideas (Laufer & Paribakht, 1998). When appropriately orchestrated, the teacher can assume the role of facilitator and monitor during the tossed terms process.

Like all engaging strategies, tossed terms provides students a novel context within which to reinforce new understandings (Kojic-Sabo & Lightbown, 1999). Terms and ideas that might otherwise be presented to them through worksheets and review sheets are literally inscribed on the six surfaces of a small box and then pitched back and forth among small groups of students in a tight circle. The terms on the box serve as prompts for questions and recalling important content.

STEP-BY-STEP

The steps described here begin with how to construct tossed terms boxes and conclude with ways they can be used most effectively for student-to-student review.

1. Begin by locating several hand-sized square boxes. These are most readily obtained from arts and crafts stores or department stores. They can even be made from existing pieces of cardboard, though this is a more time-consuming process.
2. Secure the seams of the boxes with tape to make the boxes sturdy and keep them from opening while being tossed.
3. If the box has writing and product labels on its surface, you may want to cover it with plain construction or poster paper. In order to save time and produce several finished boxes at a time, teachers have often enlisted the help of their students in steps 2 and 3.
4. Using a finished box that is secured with tape and has clean surfaces, attach typewritten text of critical content or process terms (or write directly on the box). Content terms include specific key vocabulary from the material, such as *deltoid, bicep,* and *steroid* from physical education. These boxes are useful for reviewing a prescribed set of terms and concepts. Process terms include words such as *analyze, describe, contrast, exemplify,* and *compare.* Boxes with these words can be used across topics. Both types allow review of what was learned and encourage meaningful ways of thinking about what was learned.
5. Consider ways of reusing boxes. Disciplinary teachers have devised simple adaptations to tossed terms boxes that allow them to hold any words. For instance, plastic sleeves can be taped to each surface and flash cards with review terms inserted. When review of these words is no longer necessary, they can be taken out and replaced by new ones.

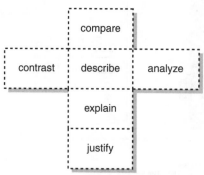

Figure 44.1 Tossed Terms Box

6. Once tossed terms boxes are made and appropriate terms attached, written, or inserted, students are ready to review with them.
7. Form small groups of no more than four students. Be sure students cluster in a tight circle so boxes do not have to be thrown but simply tossed a short distance.
8. Review the process for using the boxes with students. Typically, with content vocabulary, one student tosses the box to another and the word facing up must be defined, used in a sentence, or explained relative to the content material just learned. The other group members hold each other accountable for accuracy. With process terms, on the other hand, the word facing up serves as a prompt for a question about the content (see Figure 44.1). For example, if the word *compare* pops up and types of clouds has just been learned in a science class, the student might be asked to "Compare the formation of stratus clouds with cumulous ones." As the answer is given, the other group members pay attention for accuracy and make corrections if necessary.
9. Continue this process for as long as the review is helpful. It will be important to monitor the groups to ensure they remain on task and to clarify any misconceptions. Remember, vocabulary research makes clear that students need multiple exposures to words and concepts before developing meaningful and long-lasting understandings of them (Nagy & Scott, 2000).

APPLICATION AND EXAMPLES

A math teacher has designed a creative use of tossed terms boxes. Using a box with mathematical process terms (see Figure 44.2) and another box with numbers, students compete in teams to solve various problems.

Teams comprised of four students each form a circle on the floor with space large enough in the middle to roll the boxes like dice. Someone from Team 1 begins by rolling both boxes. A number and a process term come up. That student then calls on an individual from the other team to use the process and number to solve a problem. For example, when the number *x* (unknown) and the term *solve* showed up together, Team 2 had to solve an algebraic equation with an unknown, *x,* presented to them by Team 1. Team members can huddle and confer with one another before a spokesperson answers. If the answer is incorrect, Team 2 must roll the boxes for Team 1. Points are accumulated based on correct answers, and a team continues to answer questions and solve problems until giving an incorrect response.

An English teacher has her students work in small groups to study material from their literature anthologies using story grammar boxes. Written on their surfaces are the terms *setting, characters, conflict, resolution, theme, free question.* Students toss the box to each other and answer questions about the element that's face up for a particular story. For example, after having read "An Incident at Owl Creek Bridge" by Ambrose Bierce (1964), her students reviewed the story by recalling its critical elements. When a student caught the box and

Figure 44.2 Tossed Terms Box for Mathematics

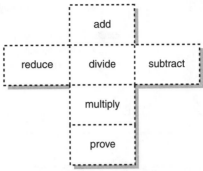

character was face up, the tosser asked: "Who is the main character of the story?" To which was replied: "An officer from the Confederate Army in the Civil War who has been captured and is being prepared to be hanged." Once the response is verified to be accurate by the other students in the group, the student answering correctly tosses the box and asks questions of someone else.

References

Bierce, A. (1964). *Ghost and horror stories by Ambrose Bierce.* Mineola, NY: Dover.

Kojic-Sabo, I., & Lightbown, P. M. (1999). Students' approaches to vocabulary learning and their relationship to success. *Modern Language Journal, 83,* 176–192.

Laufer, L., & Paribakht, T. S. (1998). The relationship between passive and active vocabularies: Effects of language learning context. *Language Learning, 48,* 365–391.

Nagy, W. E., & Scott, J. (2000). Vocabulary processes. In M. Kamil, P. Mosenthal, P. D. Pearson, & R. Barr (Eds.), *Handbook of reading research* (Vol. 3, pp. 269–284). Mahwah, NJ: Erlbaum

45

Vocabulary Cards

Learning words is time consuming and difficult for many students. In addition, most of us tire of routine vocabulary instruction. As such, teachers must find and use engaging and interesting vocabulary learning strategies that do not take a great deal of time away from reading.

Vocabulary cards are a well-researched strategy (e.g., Rekrut, 1996). When students create vocabulary cards, they begin to see the connections between words, examples of the word, nonexamples of the word, and the critical attributes associated with a word. This vocabulary strategy also helps students with their understanding of word meanings and key concepts by relating what they do not yet know to other concepts they are familiar with. The vocabulary cards require that students pay attention to words for longer periods, thus improving their memory of the words. In addition, the vocabulary cards can become an easily accessible reference for students as they can keep them on a binder ring for repeated use.

STEP-BY-STEP

Vocabulary cards are most often created on index cards, either 3 × 5 or 5 × 7 inches. The vocabulary card follows a pattern or graphic organizer. There are a number of different patterns commonly used. The traditional Frayer Model (Frayer, Frederick, & Klausmeier, 1969) can be seen in Figure 45.1. A vocabulary word card that provides students an opportunity to create graphic representation of the word is included in Figure 45.2. To use the vocabulary word cards, students should be taught the following steps:

1. Place the targeted word or concept in the middle of the graphic organizer or in the appropriate box.
2. Ask students to identify a definition—one that they can use and explain, not necessarily from the dictionary. For example, *friction* might be defined as "the resistance to movement by one thing in relation to another thing that is in contact."
3. Have the students list the characteristics or description for the word in the appropriate area. For example, the essential characteristics for the word *friction* might be: slows motion, can cause heat, associated with movement, resistance to movement.
4. Have the students then list several examples and nonexamples of the key concept. For *friction*, this could be roller coasters, rug burns, and synovial joints in humans. For nonexamples, students may identify things that reduce friction such as engine oil and objects at rest.
5. Depending on the type of vocabulary word card, students may create an illustration or visual to accompany their word.

Figure 45.1 Frayer Model Vocabulary Card

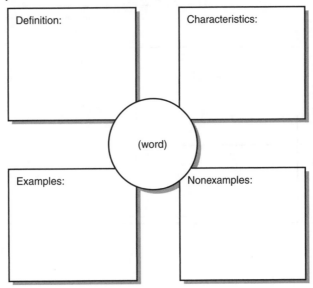

Figure 45.2 Vocabulary Card

Word	Definition
Illustration	Nonexamples

APPLICATION AND EXAMPLES

Mr. Rodriquez was concerned with the amount of lumber his students were wasting because they did not always measure correctly. He talked with his students, and read aloud from a book called *The Complete Manual of Woodworking* (Jackson, Day, & Jennings, 1996). He wanted his students to know specific terms that would ensure that they measured correctly before making the cuts to their wood. The specific terms he wanted his students to know included *length, width, height, grain, crosscut, bevel,* and *rip.*

Mr. Rodriquez required that his students create vocabulary word cards for each of these words. He quizzed each student individually by holding the vocabulary cards and asking the student to define the term, give examples, or describe the illustration. Until they could pass this quiz, the students were not allowed to use saws. As the semester progressed, Mr. Rodriquez added terms to the students' collection of vocabulary word cards. These terms included types of wood (*oak, cherry, pine*), the names of tools (*router, chisel, plane*), and more advanced woodworking terms such as *rabbet* and *spline.* A sample student vocabulary card is shown in Figure 45.3.

Figure 45.3 Vocabulary Card for Woodworking Class

Crosscut	A cut made perpendicular to the grain of a board
	Rip—to cut with the grain Mortise—to make a hole for the tenon

References

Frayer, D. A., Frederick, W. C., & Klausmeier, H. G. (1969). *A schema for testing the level of concept mastery* (Technical Report #16). Madison: University of Wisconsin, Wisconsin Center for Education Research.

Jackson, A., Day, D., & Jennings, S. (1996). *The complete manual of woodworking.* New York: Knopf.

Rekrut, M. D. (1996). Effective vocabulary instruction. *High School Journal, 80,* 66–74.

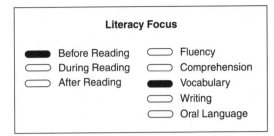

Literacy Focus

⬛ Before Reading		⬜ Fluency	
⬜ During Reading		⬜ Comprehension	
⬜ After Reading		⬛ Vocabulary	
		⬜ Writing	
		⬜ Oral Language	

Vocabulary Self-Awareness

Teaching vocabulary is complicated by the varying word knowledge levels of individual students in a given class. Students bring a range of word understanding to the task of reading. Rather than apply a "one size fits all" approach to vocabulary instruction, it is wise to assess students before the reading or other tasks involving text. This awareness is valuable for students because it highlights their understanding of what they know, as well as what they still need to learn in order to comprehend the reading.

STEP-BY-STEP

One method for accomplishing this is through *vocabulary self-awareness* (Goodman, 2001). Words are introduced at the beginning of the reading or unit, and students complete a self-assessment of their knowledge of the words (see Figure 46.1). The steps for using the vocabulary self-awareness chart include:

1. The teacher identifies target vocabulary for the lesson and provides students with a list of terms. Students may also add terms to the list as they read.
2. Each vocabulary word is rated according to the student's understanding, including an example and a definition. If they are very comfortable with the word, they give themselves a "+" (plus sign). If they think they know, but are unsure, they note the word with a "√" (check mark). If the word is new to them, they place a "−" (minus sign) next to the word.
3. Over the course of the reading or unit, students add new information to the chart. The goal is to replace all the check marks and minus signs with a plus sign. Because students continually revisit their vocabulary charts to revise their entries, they have multiple opportunities to practice and extend their growing understanding of the terms.

APPLICATION AND EXAMPLES

During a unit of study on "the life of the cell," life science teacher Jessica Smith noticed that her students were not using the unit vocabulary and were confusing important content words. She identified a number of key terms that she wanted her students to know and use as part of this unit, including *cell, chromosomes, division, haploid, homologous, meiosis, membranes, mitosis,* and *segregation.* She also asked them to record terms they were not familiar with on the self-awareness chart during their unit of study. A sample page from a student is included in Figure 46.2.

Figure 46.1 Vocabulary Self-Awareness Chart

Word	+	√	−	Example	Definition

Procedure:
1. Examine the list of words you have written in the first column.
2. Put a "+" next to each word you know well and for which you can write an accurate example and definition. Your definition and example must relate to the unit of study.
3. Place a "√" next to any words for which you can write either a definition or an example, but not both.
4. Put a "−" next to words that are new to you.

This chart will be used throughout the unit. By the end of the unit you should have the entire chart completed. Because you will be revising this chart, write in pencil.

Source: From "A Tool for Learning: Vocabulary Self-Awareness," by L. Goodman, in *Creative Vocabulary: Strategies for Teaching Vocabulary in Grades K–12* (p. 46), by C. Blanchfield (Ed.), 2001, Fresno, CA: San Joaquin Valley Writing Project. Used with permission.

Figure 46.2 Completed Vocabulary Self-Awareness Student Chart

Word	+	√	−	Example	Definition
cell	+			plant cell, animal cell, red blood cell	the basic structural and functional unit of all organisms
chromosomes		√			strands of genes contained in the nucleus of a cell
division	+			cells divide, we divide numbers	to separate into smaller units
haploid			−		

References

Goodman, L. (2001). A tool for learning: Vocabulary self-awareness. In C. Blanchfield (Ed.), *Creative vocabulary: Strategies for teaching vocabulary in grades K–12*. Fresno, CA: San Joaquin Valley Writing Project.

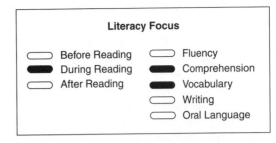

Literacy Focus

- ⬭ Before Reading
- ⬬ During Reading
- ⬭ After Reading
- ⬭ Fluency
- ⬬ Comprehension
- ⬬ Vocabulary
- ⬭ Writing
- ⬭ Oral Language

Word Grids/Semantic Feature Analysis

Word learning has once again become a "hot" topic among scholars and practitioners in literacy (Cassidy & Cassidy, 2004/2005), and for good reason. Reading for understanding is largely predicated on one's existing store of known words and strategies for constructing meanings of words from the context (Nagy & Scott, 2000). This is particularly true of reading in the disciplines, where adolescents encounter ever-increasing numbers of new words and concepts.

Several approaches to teaching vocabulary have been found to be effective (Blachowicz & Fisher, 2000), including semantic feature analysis strategies (Johnson & Pearson, 1984) or word grids (Brozo & Simpson, 2003). A word grid provides students with an organized framework for learning related terms through analysis of their similarities and differences. Building grids requires active learning, and once completed they make excellent study aids.

STEP-BY-STEP

To take full advantage of word grids they should be co-constructed with students to maximize participation in the word learning process. With this goal in mind, here are the steps for creating and using grids.

1. Start by having students participate in making a simple word grid that will serve as an example for explaining how it's constructed and used.
2. The best way to do this is to first create a premade, blank grid on an overhead transparency or PowerPoint slide, or simply draw one on the board. Notice the basic design of a word grid in Figure 47.1.
3. Then, throw out a concept or topic to students and ask them to suggest related terms. For example, the topic of "items of clothing" would elicit *shirt, shoes, pants,* and so on.

Figure 47.1 Word Grid for *Fruit*

	tree-grown	edible skin	tropical	citrus
apple	Y	Y	N	N
banana	Y	N	Y	N
grape	N	Y	N	N
orange	Y	N	Y	Y

Y = Yes
N = No

While students call out words, write them in the spaces on the left side of the grid from top to bottom.

4. Once several related terms are written along the vertical dimension of the grid, add features, characteristics, or other defining information in the spaces at the top of the grid moving left to right.

5. Finally, ask for student volunteers to help fill in the grid. Using yes/no, agree/disagree, or some other response options, connect each word with a feature. Notice in Figure 47.1 how the topic of "fruit" can easily be turned into a word grid with student help that can serve as an ideal example for explaining the process.

6. Demonstrate for students how the grid can be used to study key terminology based on critical defining characteristics. Students can be asked to provide features of similarity and difference for pairs of terms, as in "What are two common characteristics of apples and bananas?" or "Give me two ways that oranges and grapes are different."

7. After creating and analyzing a demonstration word grid, students will be much better prepared to create and study from one with actual disciplinary content.

8. Provide students a blank word grid with plenty of columns and rows for an upcoming lesson or chapter. A large version of the grid could be put on poster paper and attached to the wall, or one could be projected from an overhead or computer.

9. As critical related terms and defining information are encountered, have students write them in the grid. Invite students to suggest key terms and features, too.

10. Once the grid is complete, quiz students by asking questions about the words related to their similarities and differences. In this way, students will make a connection between the effort they put into completing and studying the grid, and the positive outcome on word knowledge quizzes.

APPLICATION AND EXAMPLES

Secondary teachers in virtually every discipline have employed word grids to help youth learn important terminology. The following grids represent the efforts of teachers and students in math (Figure 47.2), music (Figure 47.3), accounting (Figure 47.4), English (Figure 47.5), and government (Figure 47.6).

Figure 47.2 Word Grid for Geometry

	4 sides	1 pair of parallel sides	2 pairs of congruent sides	4 right angles
trapezoid				
parallelogram				
rhombus				
rectangle				
square				

Figure 47.3 Word Grid for Viols

	f-holes	soprano range	alto-tenor range	4 strings	bowed	plucked
violin						
viola						
cello						
bass						

Figure 47.4 Word Grid for Types of Taxation

	churches	businesses	individuals	schools
property				
federal—IRS				
state				
social security				
user fees				

Figure 47.5 Word Grid for Elements of Style

	rhyme	hyperbole	metaphor	allusion			author
"Ivy Crown"							Williams
"A Bird Came Down"							Dickinson
"The Road Not Taken"							Frost
"Barbie Doll"							Piercy

Figure 47.6 Word Grid for the Fifth Amendment to the U.S. Constitution

	right to remain silent	right to hold private property	right to avoid self-incrimination	doesn't apply to military cases
capital crime				
indictment				
double-jeopardy				
due process				
just compensation				

References

Blachowicz, C. L., & Fisher, P. (2000). Vocabulary instruction. In M. Kamil, P. Mosenthal, P. D. Pearson, & R. Barr (Eds.), *Handbook of reading research* (Vol. 3, pp. 503–523). Mahwah, NJ: Erlbaum.

Brozo, W. G., & Simpson, M. L. (2003). *Readers, teachers, learners: Exploring literacy across the content areas.* Upper Saddle River, NJ: Merrill/Prentice Hall.

Cassidy, J., & Cassidy, D. (2004/2005, December/January). What's hot, what's not for 2005. *Reading Today, 22*(3), 1.

Johnson, D. D., & Pearson, P. D. (1984). *Teaching reading vocabulary.* New York: Holt, Rinehart & Winston.

Nagy, W. E., & Scott, J. (2000). Vocabulary processes. In M. Kamil, P. Mosenthal, P. D. Pearson, & R. Barr (Eds.), *Handbook of reading research* (Vol. 3, pp. 269–284). Mahwah, NJ: Erlbaum.

48

Literacy Focus

- Before Reading
- During Reading
- After Reading

- Fluency
- Comprehension
- Vocabulary
- Writing
- Oral Language

Word Scavenger Hunts

If you have ever been on a scavenger hunt, then you know the excitement of finding items from a list and racing against competitors to retrieve all the items first. Scavenging for information about content area terms adds a bit of excitement to the word learning process; but more important, it can transform an otherwise predictable exercise of learning content vocabulary into an enjoyable and memorable experience for students.

As background for the strategy, consider that there are two kinds of word knowledge: definitional and contextual. Students need both kinds to really know a word. Definitional knowledge is the dictionary-like understanding of a word, which makes it possible for one to provide a terse phrase or sentence about it. Contextual knowledge, on the other hand, is the ability to make sense of a word by how it's used in print and everyday communication. Because words operate only within meaningful language contexts, some have argued that vocabulary instruction should emphasize developing word knowledge through contextual approaches (Nagy, 1997; Nagy & Stahl, 2005). Word scavenger hunts can help students develop definitional and contextual word knowledge.

STEP-BY-STEP

There are a couple of options with the word scavenger hunt strategy. One is to require students to find actual objects, pictures, and models of the words. Actual items are great to have in the learning environment, but this approach demands that youth are in possession of such items at home or have the means to obtain them. An alternative is to "even the playing field" for all students by requiring only photos and pictures in magazines from those available in the classroom. The steps below account for both approaches.

1. Begin by identifying critical terms from the content material to be covered and distribute them to each class member. It is best to limit the list to between 5–10 words.
2. Divide the class into teams of three or four. Explain how scavenger hunts work. Specify the conditions of the competition: (a) students must bring in a dictionary or glossary definition of the word on an index card; (b) they must also bring in objects and pictures that represent the words by a certain date; and (c) each team should not reveal to any other team which items were collected and where the items were found until the hunt is over.
3. If the hunt is started on Monday and concludes on Friday, allow teams to meet a couple of times during the week to update progress and revise strategy if necessary.
4. At the end of the hunt, allow teams to meet and go over their findings. Teams should share with the rest of the class the words and their definitions as well as the items found to represent the words.

5. Class members can vote on which team was most successful in the hunt. It should be at the teacher's discretion whether to provide a special reward for the best team.

6. Regardless of each team's performance, showcase student work by having teams create displays that can remain in the classroom throughout the relevant unit. Typical kinds of displays include (a) collages with index cards and pictures creatively arranged, (b) PowerPoint slide shows of definitional text and digital photos of items, and (c) display tables with actual items and definition cards.

7. If using the magazine-only approach, several of the preceding steps will not apply because the activity can be completed in one class session. Instead, students are to work together to find the best possible photo or picture that represents a word from the available magazines. An individual team can still be recognized for finding the best pictures, and collage and PowerPoint slide show options should remain, too.

APPLICATION AND EXAMPLES

For many years during the second week of the school year, an auto shop teacher had been introducing his first-year students to the internal combustion engine. His approach of requiring students to look up definitions of important related terms from a worksheet using the textbook's glossary was becoming stale. In fact, many students were so disengaged, they were not even bothering to complete the assignment. This was decidedly the wrong way to begin a class. After attending a summer professional development session in which the word scavenger hunt strategy was presented, he decided to try it as an alternative to his normal method.

When reviewing key terms to include in the hunt, the teacher discovered his old worksheet list needed updating. The new class textbook had a major section on hybrid vehicles and introduced new terms related to hybrid technology. Eventually, he settled on the following words for the hunt:

- piston
- valve
- crankshaft
- fuel injector
- spark plug
- full hybrid
- atkinson cycle
- interconverting drive train
- high-capacity battery pack

He formed four groups of four students and gave them the list of words with an explanation of the assignment. Students had 1 week to (a) write out on an index card a description of the word and its function in internal combustion, and (b) search for actual objects, models, and/or photos and illustrations of the word.

He allowed groups time to discuss the words and strategies for locating items, and gave them additional time to team up every day that week. On Friday, students brought into auto shop class the fruits of their hunt. The teacher asked each team to place its index cards and items on a designated table, then to walk around and observe what their peers had done. Finally, spokespersons from each group gave a brief report on what they learned about the words and what they found to depict the words.

Across all four groups, students were able to locate actual items for *piston, valve*, and *spark plug*. One team brought in a *crankshaft,* another had a fuel *injector.* For the hybrid terms, teams displayed various photos. Some were larger and more detailed than others, but all had found a picture to represent the three related words.

Although exhibiting a great deal of enthusiasm for the assignment, students were especially curious about where their classmates had found items. Some had items at home or were able to purchase them in an auto parts store. Others searched for them in auto junkyards. Most hybrid pictures were downloaded from the Internet or cut out of car magazines.

By the following Monday when the teacher began his unit on the internal combustion engine, students were well ahead of those from previous years. Their efforts to actively seek both definitional and contextual information about the words, left them with a more complete understanding than when the words were taught as a definitional activity only. What's more, with the students' assemblages of the actual auto parts and pictures on the tables, the teacher had ready-made examples and reminders for the key terms whenever clarification and further discussion were needed.

References

Nagy, W. (1997). On the role of context in first- and second-language vocabulary building. In N. Schmitt & M. McCarthy (Eds.), *Vocabulary: Description, acquisition, and pedagogy* (pp. 64–83). Cambridge, MA: Cambridge University Press.

Nagy, W. E., & Stahl, S. A. (2005). *Teaching word meanings*. Mahwah, NJ: Erlbaum.

49

Literacy Focus

▬ Before Reading	◯ Fluency
◯ During Reading	▬ Comprehension
◯ After Reading	▬ Vocabulary
	◯ Writing
	◯ Oral Language

Word Sorts

The ability to consider relative relationships between and among words is an important skill in acquiring vocabulary. Developing an understanding about words that are related to one another helps students develop word consciousness as well as to expand their vocabulary and content knowledge. Word sorts can provide students with a way to arrange and rearrange words in ways that mimic the critical thinking processes they use in comprehending new texts (Olle, 1994).

Sorting words involves the manipulation of a set of words, usually written on individual slips of paper, into a series of categories or related concepts. More than 25 years ago, Gillet and Temple (1978) described a process for helping students study the relationships between words. Word sorts typically consist of 10 to 20 terms and can be closed or open. Closed sorting activities are performed using categories provided by the teacher. For example, the words *chromosome, chromium*, and *chromosphere* belong in the categories, respectively, of *biology, chemistry*, and *astronomy*, which were furnished by the teacher to help students organize their understanding. An open sort is similar, but students create a set of categories to reflect their understanding of the relationships between and among a set of words. Both of these examples represent conceptual word sorts because students are using their semantic knowledge of terms. Other word sorts may focus on word patterns (e.g., words that end with *–at* and *–ag*) or derivations (words with the Latin root *nomen* or *nominis*).

STEP-BY-STEP

Word sorting is a fairly straightforward classroom procedure. Students will need instruction and modeling when they are first introduced to word sorts, but this activity can easily become a habit for students. To ensure the success of word sorting, follow these steps:

1. Model for students both open and closed sorts using content vocabulary words that they have already learned. Focus on the ways in which you made decisions about where to place a specific word. Move words from category to category to demonstrate your thinking and analysis of the word.
2. Determine if you want to use a closed or an open sort. There are benefits to both and most teachers use both regularly. Make sure that you inform students each time you use word sorts whether they will be using categories you created or categories of their own.
3. Identify 10 to 20 words that can be sorted based on the topic under investigation.
4. Copy the words and then cut the papers such that each word is on its own small piece of paper. Each student, or each pair of students, will need the complete set

of words. Many teachers have their student helpers or parent volunteers do the cutting for them.

5. Provide students time to sort the words. As they do, circulate around the room and ask them questions about their word placement choices.
6. You may want to ask students to copy their sorts into their notebooks or to write a summary of their thinking behind the sorts as they complete the task.

APPLICATION AND EXAMPLES

At the beginning of the school year, Ms. Abernathy uses an open word sort of mathematics terms to check her student understanding of the content (see Figure 49.1). This word sort allows her to identify gaps in her students' knowledge and understanding and then plan instruction. For example, when Thuy added an "e" to the end of *pi,* she knew he needed help with this concept or label. She also likes to have students explain their sorts and share with the class their decision making regarding the creation of categories and the ways in which words are organized.

Midway through the school year, she repeats this word sort to determine if there are students who still need focused instruction in some of the key terms used in mathematics. For example, when Jessica created a category "words I don't know" and included transverse in that category, it gave Ms. Abernathy information about this student's needed instruction.

Similarly, Mr. Kaufman uses the words found in Figure 49.2 to create a discussion with his science students about the ways in which we understand the disciplines of science and pseudoscience. Mr. Kaufman also uses this word sort to focus his students' attention on the

Figure 49.1 Mathematics Word Sort

sum	subtract	difference
addition	total	divide
multiply	squared	exponent
right	isosceles	transverse
equilateral	parallel	radius
diameter	circumference	pi

Figure 49.2 Word Sort for Science

astronomy	astrology	astronomer
astrolabe	astronaut	biology
biome	biosphere	biotic
chlorophyll	chloroplast	chlorella
chlorine	ecology	economy
ecosystem	ecotype	voracious
omnivore	carnivore	herbivore

prefixes and suffixes used in science. He knows that students' understanding of common affixes will help them make educated guesses about unfamiliar words when they encounter them in their readings.

References

Gillet, J. W., & Temple, C. (1978). Word knowledge: A cognitive view. *Reading World, 18,* 132–140.

Olle, R. D. (1994). Word sorts: Vocabulary development with adult literacy learners. *Journal of Reading, 38,* 230–232.

50

Literacy Focus

⬛ Before Reading	⬜ Fluency
⬜ During Reading	⬛ Comprehension
⬜ After Reading	⬛ Vocabulary
	⬜ Writing
	⬜ Oral Language

Word Walls

Word walls are alphabetically arranged (by first letter) words displayed in a manner to allow easy visual access to all students in the room (Brabham & Villaume, 2001). As Cunningham and Allington (2003) remind us, however, it is essential to "do" a word wall, not merely display one. Some teachers rely on a selection from the "500 Most Used Words List" (Harwell, 2001) of words commonly used in speaking and writing. Although they are relatively simple words, many are misapplied (*knew/new*) or misspelled (*friend, neighbor,* and *when*), leading to unclear communication.

In addition to high-frequency words, teachers also use word walls to highlight vocabulary that is related to a unit of instruction. For example, during a study of *The Grapes of Wrath* (Steinbeck, 1939), a teacher may include words like *Dust Bowl, Okies, drought,* and *migrant* on the word wall. These English teachers do the word wall through brief (10 minutes or so) daily instruction around a particular set of words. Typically, five words are introduced and located on the word wall display. Novel games such as Guess the Covered Word (Cunningham & Allington, 2003), where a word is revealed one letter at a time, may be used. It is important that the words, once taught, remain in the same spot so students can reliably locate them. Typically, students are held accountable for word wall words and are expected to regularly use them and spell them correctly.

STEP-BY-STEP

1. Make a decision about the type of words you will use with your word wall. You may choose to select words that are frequently misspelled and misused, or perhaps words related to the content you are teaching. Content words may be organized by topic and unit, or can be derived from Latin and Greek root words. For example, a science teacher may select words with a *bio–* root that include *biology, abiotic,* and *biopsy.*
2. Identify a location in your room for the word wall display. The area should be easily seen, so consider the sight line of a seated student. Many classrooms do not have a large open wall so don't rule out unconventional areas such as the space between the board and ceiling.
3. Decide how you will affix the words to the surface. We like reusable adhesive because it will not mark walls. The words will be rearranged as new words are added, so this method makes it a simple proposition.
4. Determine how you will visually organize your word wall. Because it is arranged in alphabetical order, large letters should be prominently displayed to allow for a visual reference. The words need to be laid out in an organized fashion, so plan for a simple grid pattern. Some letters of the alphabet are infrequently used and you may want to

Figure 50.1 Word Wall Grid

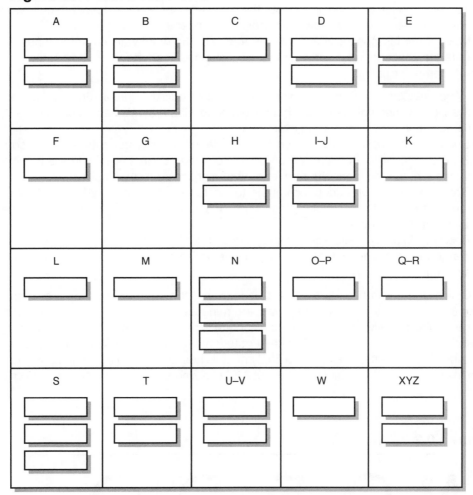

collapse these into categories. A sample grid for a classroom word wall appears in Figure 50.1.

5. Words should be printed with large block letters on white cards no smaller than 4 × 6 inches. Sentence strips can be printed using the envelope setting on your printer. Experiment with a few sizes and colors to determine the best combination for viewing from any point in the room.

6. The word wall always begins as a blank canvas. Start the word wall with your students by explaining the purpose and use. Introduce a few words at a time so that they can learn them well. As new words appear on the word wall, rearrange them so that they remain in alphabetical order within the category. This allows students to scan efficiently while reinforcing organizational skills.

7. Use your word wall daily. Remind students that these "no excuse" words should be spelled correctly all the time in written work. As you teach, refer to words displayed on the wall. Word wall games like Guess the Covered Word can fill a few minutes at the end of class. Be sure to include words from previous lessons as well.

APPLICATION AND EXAMPLES

The word wall in Ms. Jackson's eighth-grade algebra class has been a source of information and fun since the beginning of the year. She displays content words related to the units of instruction, introducing new vocabulary as it is needed. Therefore, her word wall contains words such as *exponent* and *variable.* Ms. Jackson avoids using more than five words at a time, as she has noticed from past lessons that this is cognitive overload. Because she doesn't care for her own handwriting, she prints the words on sentence strips. "I think it works out better this way—the words show up better," she observes.

Most of her lessons include a few minutes with the word wall to reinforce new learning and reiterate concepts from earlier in the year. She has a repertoire of short activities to play with students, including:

- *Word Call Out:* She calls out a word and students quickly write a sentence containing the word. When finished, students raise a hand. She draws a name and awards participation points for correct examples.
- *Guess My Word:* Ms. Jackson provides the definition, and students write the correct word on a small whiteboard. When she announces "Boards up!," she scans the room to see who understands the term and who might need further instruction.
- *Flashlight:* Teams of students compete to locate words on the word wall. Ms. Jackson turns off the lights in the room, then asks for a word by its definition. Teams shine their lights on the correct word.
- *Read My Mind:* Ms. Jackson provides clues about how the term is used in mathematics. Students write down guesses until a student announces the correct answer.

One of the advantages of these activities is that they don't require a lot of preparation. "I like using these when we have a few spare minutes, or as a warm-up to get them going," she says. Occasionally, she uses a more elaborate activity for review. In the days leading up to a test, Ms. Jackson plays WORDO with her students (Cunningham & Hall, 1998). She distributes a blank grid like the one in Figure 50.2 and tells her students to fill in each box with words from the word wall. "Don't just pick the first 24," she warns them, "choose words from all over

Figure 50.2 WORDO Card

W	O	R	D	O
		FREE SPACE		

the word wall." After several minutes, each has a unique board filled with mathematical terms. Like the familiar game of Bingo, she picks words written on index cards and calls them out.

"*Y*-intercept," she calls, and students rapidly scan their WORDO boards in the hope of crossing out this term. "Who's got a definition?" she asks.

Carlos responds, "It's the point on a graph."

"Yes, but there's more to it than that. Someone build on Carlos's answer."

Lisette offers, "It's the point where the graph incepts the *y*-axis."

"Right! Well done, both of you," Ms. Jackson says.

This continues—they usually play Blackout (all the squares on a board are filled), and in keeping with the fun, Ms. Jackson provides small prizes for winners. "Really, we're all winners," she remarks later. "I get to review terms, and they see it as a fun way to spend 20 minutes."

References

Brabham, E. G., & Villaume, S. K. (2001). Building walls of words. *The Reading Teacher, 54,* 700–702.

Cunningham, P. M., & Allington, R. L. (2003). *Classrooms that work: They can all read and write* (3rd ed.). Boston: Allyn & Bacon.

Cunningham, P. M., & Hall, D. P. (1998). *Month by month phonics for upper grades: A second chance for struggling readers and students learning English.* Greensboro, NC: Carson-Dellosa.

Harwell, J. M. (2001). *Complete learning disabilities handbook: Ready-to-use strategies and activities for teaching students with learning disabilities* (2nd ed.). Paramus, NJ: Center for Applied Research in Education.

Steinbeck, J. (1939). *Grapes of wrath.* New York: Viking Press.